MEDITATION

DAVID FONTANA is Distinguished Visiting Fellow at the University of Wales, Cardiff, holds Professorships at two Portugese universities and is fellow of the British Psychological Society. He lectures widely in the US, Europe, Middle East and India and is the author of numerous highly acclaimed books, translated into twenty three languages. These include: *New Perspectives: Dreams, The Meditator's Handbook, Teaching Meditation to Children, Growing Together, Know Who You Are, Be What You Want* and *The Lotus In The City*.

THE SERIES

New Perspectives provide attractive and accessible introductions to a comprehensive range of mind, body and spirit topics. Beautifully designed and illustrated, these practical books are written by experts in each subject.

Titles in the series include:

ALEXANDER TECHNIQUE
by Richard Brennan

AROMATHERAPY
by Christine Wildwood

DREAMS
by David Fontana

FENG SHUI
by Man-Ho Kwok with Joanne O'Brien

FLOWER REMEDIES
by Christine Wildwood

HOMEOPATHY
by Peter Adams

MASSAGE
by Stewart Mitchell

MEDITATION
by David Fontana

NLP
by Carol Harris

NUMEROLOGY
by Rodford Barrat

REFLEXOLOGY
by Inge Dougans

TAROT
by A T Mann

New Perspectives

MEDITATION

An Introductory Guide to Relaxation for Mind and Body

DAVID FONTANA

Shaftesbury, Dorset • Boston, Massachusetts

Melbourne, Victoria

First published as *The Elements of Meditation* in 1991
by Element Books Limited

This revised edition first published in Great Britain in 1999 by
Element Books Limited, Shaftesbury, Dorset SP7 8BP

Published in the USA in 1999 by Element Books, Inc.
160 North Washington Street, Boston, MA 02114

Published in Australia in 1999 by
Element Books and distributed by
Penguin Australia Limited
487 Maroondah Highway,
Ringwood, Victoria 3134

Designed for Element Books Limited by
Design Revolution, Queens Park Villa,
30 West Drive, Brighton, East Sussex BN2 2GE

ELEMENT BOOKS LIMITED
Editorial Director: Sarah Sutton
Editorial Manager: Jane Pizzey
Commissioning Editor: Grace Cheetham
Production Director: Roger Lane

DESIGN REVOLUTION
Editorial Director: Ian Whitelaw
Art Director: Lindsey Johns
Editor: Kay MacMullan
Designer: Vanessa Good

Printed and bound in Great Britain by
Bemrose Security Printing, Derby

British Library Cataloguing in Publication
data available

Library of Congress Cataloging in Publication data available

ISBN 1-86204-627-1

CONTENTS

ACKNOWLEDGEMENTS

Dedicating this book to any of those who have helped my meditation practices might be presumptuous, in that it would imply their support for all I have written. This would be inappropriate. Instead I gratefully acknowledge their wisdom, in particular that of John Crook, Lama Damcho Yonten, Lama Yeshe Dorje, Lama Chhimed Rigdzin Rinpoche, Lama Sogyal Rinpoche, Ngakpa Chögyam, Reverend Master Daishin Morgan, Godwin Sararatne, Manny Patel, and Flo Farmer. And since books have been so important in my life, I feel honoured also to acknowledge those teachers such as Eugen Herrigel, Lama Govinda, John Blofeld and Charles Luk, whom I never met, but who are nevertheless intimate friends.

BEGINNING THE JOURNEY

CHAPTER ONE

MANY WAYS OF TRAVELLING

There are many ways of travelling. When we are very small we travel by crawling. Then we learn to stand and to take our first few steps. Then we learn to walk, later, we take to bicycles, and then to cars and trains and boats and even to aeroplanes. Distances that to our ancestors would have seemed unimaginable are covered at great speed. In the modern world, so much of our life is bound up with movement. We rarely stay for long in the same place. With a kind of restless energy we are forever just passing through, forever on the way to somewhere else, forever in transit, forever ready to depart.

But there is another way of travelling. A way of travelling that begins when we first open our eyes on the world, and that continues until we draw our last breath.

This is an inner way of travelling that takes us through our own minds. A journey made not by boats and planes but by thoughts and feelings. A journey involving both the routine of daily life and the magical flights of our own imagination. A journey that transports us through a vast sweep of feelings and emotions, from dizzy heights to bitter depths. A journey that we have no

LEFT BY CLOSING OUR EYES WE CAN BEGIN TO EXPLORE WHAT IS GOING ON IN OUR OWN MINDS WITHOUT THE INTERFERENCE OF THE MANY DISTRACTIONS AROUND US.

8

option but to take, since it is the journey of being fully alive, and of being who we truly are.

Stop reading for a moment and just think about this journey. Close your eyes. How does it feel to be alive, to be in your own mind, without the distractions of what you can hear and see?

Usually we are so occupied by the outside world that we never stop to think that what is real is what happens inside our minds. The outer world of colours and shapes and people and objects only exists for us when we have registered it in our minds, when we have filtered it through our senses and recognized and interpreted it in our own minds.

We become so accustomed to recognizing and interpreting the things that we see, that we forget that we are doing it. We forget that things are not real for us until we've taken them into our mind. We rarely look into our minds, into our own being. We are always looking outwards, as if the objects around us can actually create our experience by themselves, as if our experience of life is created by an outer magic rather than by our own senses and our own minds.

LOST IN THOUGHT

'But', you may argue, 'I'm always listening to my mind. That's half my trouble. I'm constantly lost in thought instead of concentrating on what I'm supposed to be doing.' Yes all right. But to be lost in thought is simply concentrating on the links within our mind that start at one point and meander off into the distance until we can't even remember where our starting point was. This isn't listening to your mind. It's giving in to the chatter in our mind, the unwanted thoughts that we have to listen to whether we like it or not. This chatter constantly reminds us of our worries, our depressions, our jealousies, our grievances, our angers. It allows us to remember happy memories one moment, only to sadden us the next by reminding us that those happy times are past. It makes us dream up imaginary disasters, to go over and over a painful time we've just had with someone, to

BELOW OUR MINDS TEND TO FLIT FROM ONE THING TO ANOTHER – WE START ONE JOB AND BREAK OFF HALF-WAY THROUGH AS WE REMEMBER OTHER THINGS WE SHOULD BE DOING.

rehearse endlessly what we should have said to them if only we'd thought of it in time. This chatter within our minds has us so completely at its mercy that we begin to wonder 'Who's in charge here?'

The same lack of control applies to our feelings. Emotions arise whether we want them to or not. We feel happy or sad, angry or frightened, contented or discontented, attracted or repelled, patient or impatient, interested or bored, as if we have no say at all in the matter.

But it gets worse. For even when we are looking out on to the world, most of the time we aren't paying proper attention. We look at or listen to something and then almost immediately switch to looking at or listening to something else. We start a job and break off half-way through as we remember other things we should be doing at the same time. We have an object in our hands, put it down, and a moment later can't remember where we've put it. We hear something and after a short while we've forgotten what it was. Our minds flit endlessly from one thing to another, and then we blame our failure to get anything done on our poor memories, or on other people or on our hectic lives.

Does it have to be like this? Are we made in such a way that our minds – and therefore our lives – must always be beyond our control and understanding? Or is there some way in which we can regain control and understanding – and become more aware of who we really are?

TRANSFORMING THE JOURNEY

The answer is that no, it doesn't have to be like this; and yes, there is a way in which we can take control and begin to understand what goes on in our minds, and become more our own man or woman. Which brings me back full circle to the idea of travelling. We are already part of the way along our journey of experiencing our own lives, but what we can do is to take more control over the direction that the journey takes.

If we wish – and remember that the choice is always our own – we can begin to change the journey so that we are no longer confused, but are free to see what is going on. It can be rather like washing the sleep from our eyes and seeing for the first time the beauty of the landscape through which we are passing. We can learn to read the signals and the signposts that are all around us, and decide where we want to go instead of being carried along helplessly like a leaf in the wind.

How is this done?

As is often the way with seemingly difficult questions, the answer is in fact very simple. By simple, however, I do not mean easy. If we think it is easy, one of two things is likely to happen:

1   We will give up when we find that we were wrong, or

2   We will carry on, but begin to believe that it is difficult –
    this may make us determined to succeed, but this same
    determination could cause us to fail.

For the answer to how we can change our journey through life is meditation, and meditation should be practised as if it were a bird we are holding in our hands. Hold it too casually and the bird flies away. Hold it too tightly and the bird is smothered. Hold it neither casually nor tightly, and the bird rests in our hands and charms us with its singing.

In terms of our journey, what this means is that if we walk carelessly, taking no notice of where we are or what is around us, we lose our way; and if we walk along fixed in our beliefs, with our heads down instead of watching out for the signposts, we lose our way just as surely, and often end up wandering even further from the path.

MEDITATION

The next question of course is 'what is meditation?'.

The word comes from the Latin *meditari*, which means 'frequent'. Meditation is therefore something that is done frequently. So we know how often we do it, but this still doesn't tell us what it is that we actually do.

In fact it is quite useful that the word 'meditation' does not tell us exactly what it is, because this gives us some freedom of choice. It allows us to set out on our journey without too many fixed ideas in our head. It allows us to travel, but does not tell us where we have to start from, how we have to travel, or where we have to go. It makes us no false promises and asks nothing of us except that we ask something of ourselves.

So meditation is not a set of beliefs that you have to follow. Followers of particular schools of meditation or particular spiritual or occult traditions may tell you that theirs is the best way, and that any other way is 'wrong'. Yet if you listen to the founders of these traditions rather than to the followers, you will find that usually they said no such thing. They taught a way, a path, but they rarely criticized other paths. And if you take the trouble to look at each of these different paths you will find that in the distance, higher up the mountain, they seem to meet and become one, though where this one path goes afterwards you will have in the fullness of time to discover for yourself.

LEFT THERE ARE MANY DIFFERENT WAYS TO MEDITATE. NO ONE METHOD IS ACTUALLY BETTER THAN ANOTHER.

12

REASONS FOR MEDITATING

Before you start on the journey of meditation (or even if you are already well advanced on that journey) it is good to pause and think about why you are interested in it.

Perhaps you have heard that meditation can make you calmer, more peaceful, less anxious.

Perhaps you have heard that it brings physical benefits, like lowering of the blood pressure, or protection against heart disease and stress-related illnesses.

Perhaps you have heard that it will bring blissful states of mind, or give you psychic powers, or make you happy, or even bring you to enlightenment.

Perhaps you have heard it will help you give up drugs, or deepen your powers of concentration, or develop your creativity, or make you more loving towards yourself and others.

Perhaps you have heard it will help keep you young, or help you live longer, or cure insomnia, or help to control pain.

Perhaps you have heard it will make you more intelligent or more beautiful or more powerful or bring success or make you wise.

Or perhaps you are intrigued by pictures of people sitting cross-legged, gazing into inner space, and wonder what they are seeing.

Look carefully at these motives, not because any one of them is right and all the others wrong, but simply so that, after noting them, you can allow yourself to put them gently to one side. Meditation may indeed bring you these things, some of them or all of them.

But you will travel more surely if you begin your journey, your practice of meditation, with a mind that is concerned less with what you will achieve than with what you are doing.

With this attitude of mind, meditation is looked upon as a teacher rather than as a servant. For meditation, though it never tells you what to do, will not be told what to do either. If you set out on your journey with an imaginary travel ticket in your hands, your destination marked clearly and everything guaranteed – and with a return ticket as well so that you can come back if you don't like it when you get there – then not only will you fail to arrive where you want to be, you will risk failing even to leave your starting point.

DESCRIPTIONS OF MEDITATION

One of the best descriptions of meditation is

'just sitting'
or
'sitting quietly doing nothing'.

If this suggests meditation is non-activity, or non-doing, then this is partly true. Because although much of our meditation is done while we sit quietly, the benefits of meditation carry over into our everyday life, no matter how active.

Think of meditation therefore in terms of what you are doing rather than of what you are achieving.

Think of it as something that allows you to see more clearly what is going on inside yourself, in your own mind, in your own body.

And think of it as a process that allows you also to see more clearly what is going on in the outside world.

THE BENEFITS OF MEDITATION

I have already said that you should avoid viewing any of the benefits of meditation as your 'goal'. It is better to appreciate them if they occur...and then continue with your practice.

There is however a mounting body of research and of clinical reports that point to a wide range of benefits that can follow from regular meditation. These include:

a decrease in
- tension and anxiety
- stress-related physical problems such as high blood pressure, palpitations and abnormal heart rhythms, insomnia, stuttering, and tension headaches
- drug addiction and drug dependence
- depression, irritability and other negative psychological states.

and an increase in
- feelings of peace, optimism, and self-worth
- creativity, efficiency, productivity and energy
- emotional release, spontaneity and contact with emotional life
- openness to the unconscious and to repressed memories, hopes and so on
- independence, self-discipline and sense of identity.

There is also evidence that meditation can improve memory, concentration, attention span, patience and evenness of temper. Some studies have also shown it can be useful in the management of chronic pain.

15

Exercise 1

Even if you have already done some meditation, this exercise is still of great value. For the moment, don't concern yourself with posture or breathing. These are important issues in meditation, but for now, concentrate simply on this one task.

Sit comfortably, in a quiet place where you are unlikely to be disturbed. If you have a telephone, take it off the hook. Now close your eyes, and think quite simply about 'me'.

Don't ask any direct questions about yourself, or try to judge or describe yourself in any way. Just concentrate on being 'me' and on what 'me' is experiencing at this moment. Be aware of what 'me' is feeling, whether it be thoughts, emotions, bodily sensations, sounds, or whatever. What you are doing is being conscious of what it is to be 'me'. The 'me-ness of me' if you like. Don't try to hang on to any of the things 'me' is experiencing. Simply observe them, from a distance if you can.

Continue with this exercise for a few minutes (the actual length of time is unimportant) until you feel you have learnt from it, then open your eyes.

What was it you learnt?
Don't worry if it is difficult to put it into words.

Maybe it was simply the experience of being aware of yourself as a living being, with bodily sensations and with a stream of thoughts running through your head.

Maybe you realized how little control you actually have at this moment over your thoughts.

Maybe you realized that thoughts seem to arise from some unknown depth inside yourself, and that you have no idea where they come from and how they form.

Maybe you recognized that, in the midst of all these thoughts and feelings and bodily sensations, it is very difficult to know where (and who and what) 'me' really is.

Maybe you recognized that life – and being alive – is a very mysterious business, one that normally we take completely for granted, but which in moments like this, we recognize as unfathomably strange.

Or maybe it was something personal, and none of these things.

No matter. The important point is that this exercise is the beginning of the journey inwards, a journey that takes us not to another country but to a place where we are and have always been, and helps us, as the poet T.S.Eliot puts it,

'to know it for the first time'.

Carl Jung, the great Swiss psychologist, once said that we have no idea where the mind ends. He was right, meditation helps us explore some of this unknown vastness within ourselves.

Meditation allows you, once it has helped you reach something that looks like a goal, to see more clearly and to realize that the goal is not the end of the journey. Other goals lie beyond, and other goals beyond them too, so much so that you may realize that the meditation itself is the goal, and be content with that until you come to realize that even that is not the whole of the truth.

This a good point at which to try Exercise 1.

THE KINGDOM OF THE MIND

By practising Exercise 1 you have already 'become' a meditator. And you can repeat Exercise 1 several times over the course of the next few days before you go on to Exercise 2.

There are no set rules. If you listen to yourself, you will soon get an idea of the pace at which you should be travelling through each of the exercises contained in this book. The only guideline is that there are no prizes for travelling quickly. Time means little in work of this kind. Rush ahead too eagerly, and you will soon find the need to go back and retrace some of your early steps. Travel at the right speed, however, and each step will take you, surely and steadily, to the next one.

You still may find the need to retrace your steps from time to time. We never, in a way, outgrow the earlier exercises as we pass on to the later ones. In some ways all meditation, no matter how advanced it may be, is simply the act, as in Exercise 1, of sitting down and seeing – and being – who you are.

LEFT TIME IS UNIMPORTANT WHEN IT COMES TO THE JOURNEY OF MEDITATION. IN FACT THE FASTER YOU TRY TO TRAVEL, THE LONGER IT WILL TAKE YOU TO REACH YOUR DESTINATION.

The journey of meditation does not take place in a straight line nor at an even pace. We move in and out of experiences rather like a path winds its way up the wooded slopes of a mountain, sometimes appearing to double back, sometimes rising steeply, sometimes gently and slowly.

In meditation you are travelling through the kingdom of your mind. We all live in a rich and beautiful kingdom, full of enchanted beauty. The tragedy is that we rarely stir out of the one small village. We have only the haziest notion that outside our single village street there are roads stretching away into the distance, there are open fields, broad rivers, tall trees, secret places, snow-capped mountains, a magical landscape under a clear and welcoming sky.

You have now made your first move out into that country. There are two wise sayings from the East that will help you on your travels. Take them with you, and study them from time to time. The first saying invites you to:

'start and continue'.

The second reminds you that a:

'journey of a thousand miles begins with the first step'.

These sayings remind us that nothing can be accomplished unless we are prepared to take the first step. And once the first step is behind us, we can move on to the next. And thus, step by step, we make progress. Start ... and then continue.

FINDING THE TIME

CHAPTER TWO

In making any journey, we have to take decisions about timing, about the best time for travelling and about how long we want to spend on the road. This is also true for the journey of meditation. Decisions about timing are particularly important on the journey of meditation because they require us to be disciplined and to keep to some kind of schedule.

THE BENEFITS OF DAILY PRACTICE

As a meditator, you should be setting aside a period of time for daily practice. A short period each day is much better than a lengthy period once a week (or whenever we feel like it). Daily practice ensures that:

- The mind and body quickly get into the habit of carrying out the task concerned.
- Mind and body have less time to 'forget' the progress they have made.
- Family and friends come to realize that there is a set time each day when you don't want to be disturbed.
- You become more committed to your practice – and to your continuing practice.
- You begin to think of yourself as a meditator.

JANUARY

7 Monday 9am Jessica school Awards
~~10am Meditation~~ Call Reflexologist to make an appointment.
3pm Steven Dentist

18 Tuesday 2pm Gym?
~~10am Meditation~~
11am Coffe morning at nursery
12 o'clock Pick Jessica up from school

19 Wednesday 7am Plumber due to check boiler!!!!
shop for dinn
~~10am Meditation~~
8am Pauline to take Jessica to school on

20 Thursday 8am Pick up Sophie and take Jessica
9am Hairdressers 2pm New Yoga Class
~~10am meditation~~ 8pm Cinema

21 Friday ~~10am Meditation~~
9am Steven's school play
8pm Parents evening Buy flowers for

22 Saturday 3pm Massage
9am Jessica Ballet 6pm Drop childre
~~10am Meditation~~ 7.30pm Dinner
2pm Steven and Paul Football

23 Sunday ~~10am Meditation~~
4pm Mum's for tea

AUGUST

19 Monday
8.30am Breakfast meeting with Georg
2pm Meeting at headoffice
~~5pm meditate~~ phone dentist

20 Tuesday 5am Meeting – leave at six!
12 o'clock lunch with Simon
~~5pm Meditate~~ 7pm Golf

21 Wednesday
Prepare quotes
7.30pm dinner with Julie
~~5pm meditate~~

22 Thursday
8am Deadline for quote
11am Car service 8pm Supermarket
7pm Collect car ~~5pm meditate~~

23 Friday
DAY OFF ~~5pm meditate~~

24 Saturday
12 o'clock meet Simon in pub
2pm Football ~~5pm meditate~~
9.30pm Party!!!

25 Sunday
12 o'clock lunch at Barts
3pm Cinema ~~5pm meditate~~

APRIL

12 Monday 9am Temp due day free
to show her the ropes
Mr Brown out all day
call Hotel and give them final numbers
☒ 6pm MEDITATION for dinner guests ●

13 Tuesday
Collect traveller's cheques Final dress fitting
Pick up tickets
for Honeymoon ☒ 6pm MEDITATION ●
7.30pm keep fit ●

14 Wednesday 8am Pay florist on way to work
9am Phone bestman and check
he's done the speech!!!
5pm Hair appointment ☒ 6pm MEDITATION
with headress – don't forget

15 Thursday Finish work today
1 o'clock Lunch at pub with the girls
☒ 6pm MEDITATION
8pm Girlie night in with Bridesmaids

16 Friday Collect flowers for mums
1 o'clock lunch with the in-laws
3pm Collect dress from seamstress
☒ 6pm MEDITATION 5pm Early night ●

17 Saturday
2pm Wedding
☒ 6pm MEDITATION ●

18 Sunday 2pm Honeymoon Check in at 10am
5pm Arrive at hotel for fly at mid-day
☒ 6pm MEDITATION

21

ABOVE ONLY BY PRACTISING EVERY DAY, WILL YOU REAP THE FULL BENEFITS OF MEDITATION. THE HABIT WILL INCREASE YOUR COMMITMENT AND YOU WILL FIND THAT OTHERS RESPECT THIS TOO.

It is also best to set aside the same time of day in which to carry out your daily practice. This again helps to build up the idea of routine. In a short while you will find that when the time for daily meditation approaches, your mind will turn to the practice, and that if for some reason you can't meditate at this time you will feel that something is missing.

RIGHT MANY PEOPLE CHOOSE TO MEDITATE AT THE END OF THE DAY, AS THEY FIND THAT THIS HELPS THEM TO SLEEP PEACEFULLY.

LEFT CHOOSE YOUR MEDITATION TIME ACCORDING TO YOUR
LIFESTYLE AND OWN INTERNAL CLOCK.

You should choose the time of day at which you want to meditate carefully. Many people recommend first thing in the morning, while others prefer last thing at night. Early morning has its advantages, because the mind is (in theory!) clear, and the meditation gets the day off to a good start. On the other hand last thing at night helps to calm down the mind, and can give you a good night's sleep. Midday, when your body may be at its peak, also has its advantages.

WHICH TIME IS BEST FOR YOU?

Before deciding on what is best for you, think about your personal situation and your own biological rhythms. Some people feel at their best in the mornings, but find it a major struggle to keep awake in the evenings. Other people find they never feel properly awake until after breakfast, while at night their minds are open and clear. You can always change your mind later if things don't work out.

Do be clear from the start, however, that meditation is not about falling asleep; nor is it about struggling to keep awake. In meditation the mind should be relaxed but alert, concentrated and focused, rather than woolly and sluggish. So try to pick a time when sleepiness isn't a major problem.

HOW MANY TIMES A DAY?

People sometimes ask whether they should aim for two sessions of meditation a day (morning and evening perhaps) rather than just one. Do double sessions bring double benefits? They may well do, but don't be over-ambitious. Think about what is practical for you. One

ABOVE FAMILY COMMITMENTS MAY PLAY A LARGE PART IN YOUR DECISION ABOUT WHEN TO MEDITATE. IT IS ALSO
IMPORTANT THAT YOU DO NOT CHOOSE A TIME OF DAY WHEN YOUR ARE TIRED AND YOUR MIND IS NOT ALERT.

short period of meditation a day that leaves you feeling you want to do more, is much better than two longer periods that leave you feeling the whole business is becoming a bind. There are people who meditate regularly twice a day, for an hour each time, but they have usually worked up to this over many months and even years. To begin with, settle for once a day, at a convenient time, and promise yourself that you will try to keep this up regularly for a set period of time.

A month is a useful starter, but if even this sounds too much for you a fortnight is enough to be going on with. Even a week will give you something of the 'feel' of meditation, and will in all probability inspire you to add another week, and then another. Soon your practice will have become so much a part of your life that you will be able to forget about your weekly targets. Meditation will become something you do automatically, like taking a shower or walking the dog.

APRIL						
Mon	**Tues**	**Wed**	**Thurs**	**Fri**	**Sat**	**Sun**
Drop-in meditation class **29**	**30**	Start 4 week **31** meditation course	meditation at home once a day **1**	meditation at home once a day **2**	meditation at home once a day **3**	meditation at home once a day **4**
meditation at home once a day **5**	meditation at home once a day **6**	meditation course **7**	meditation at home once a day **8**	meditation at home once a day **9**	meditation at home once a day **10**	meditation at home once a day **11**
meditation at home once a day **13**	meditation at home once a day **14**	meditation course **15**	meditation at home once a day **16**	meditation at home once a day **17**	meditation at home once a day **18**	meditation at home once a day **19**
meditation at home once a day **20**	meditation at home once a day **21**	meditation course **22**	meditation at home once a day **23**	meditation at home once a day **24**	meditation at home once a day **25**	meditation at home once a day **26**
meditation at home once a day **27**	meditation at home once a day **28**	meditation course **29**	**30**			

ABOVE AT THE OUTSET YOU MAY CHOOSE TO SET YOURSELF A TARGET FOR REGULAR MEDITATION. THIS CAN BE A WEEK, TWO WEEKS OR A MONTH – WHATEVER YOU FEEL COMFORTABLE WITH.

FITTING IN YOUR MEDITATION

Another question often asked by beginners is, does it matter if you can't meditate every day? For example, you may meditate in the evening and know that every Saturday night you go out until late. Having missed your meditation time, you know you are unlikely to meditate once you get home. So what do you do? Give up the meditation once a week, or give up your Saturday night?

The answer is that meditation must be part of your routine, but that you do have some flexibility. In the early weeks and months of your meditation practice you should not change your life too much in order to fit in your meditation. If you do, it is likely to become a bind. It's no surprise that many people who rush headlong into meditation and tell everyone around them how wonderful it is, are soon found to have given it up altogether. However adaptable and dedicated you are, or may think you are, it is still best to change your routines gradually. Organizing your whole life around meditation is one of the quickest ways of ensuring that you will drop the practice soon after starting.

So keep your Saturday night out. But – and it is an important but – try on Saturday to do a short meditation of a different kind at some

WHAT MEDITATION ISN'T – AND IS

Many people have false ideas about what meditation is. Beginners often ask 'How do I know I'm meditating?' So, let's sort out some of the things meditation is and isn't.

Meditation isn't:
- Falling asleep.
- Going into a trance.
- Shutting yourself off from reality and becoming unworldly.
- Being selfish.
- Doing something 'unnatural'.
- Becoming lost in thought.
- Forgetting where you are.

Meditation is:
- Keeping the mind alert and attentive.
- Keeping the mind focused and concentrated.
- Becoming more aware of the world.
- Becoming more human.
- Knowing where you are.

I am often asked if meditation is like hypnosis. In fact the two could hardly be more different. Hypnosis is a drowsy, almost drugged state, whereas meditation is about being more aware. Both can be described as pleasant, but there the similarity between them ends.

I'm also asked whether meditation is an 'altered state of consciousness'. In a sense, yes it is, although it would be more accurate to describe it as a rediscovery of one's 'normal' state of consciousness, the state of awareness that we would have were it not for the distractions that dominate our lives.

> If your mind is really in the alert yet relaxed state of meditation, you will find that even if you feel sleepy when you begin your practice, it will soon pass. There is even some medical evidence that meditation rests and restores both body and mind more fully even than sleep itself.

other time during the day. You could try meditation that doesn't involve sitting (*see* chapter 3). This not only helps to keep your practice regular but also gives you an opportunity to broaden your practice, so that one day you will be able to undertake it whenever you wish and wherever you are.

While we are on the subject of nights out, it's important to say that taking up meditation shouldn't take you from your friends. To begin with, they will probably regard you as a little odd, and you may before long begin to make a new circle of friends from amongst other meditators. But your friends are your friends, and it is foolish to change them just so that you can meditate.

Certainly change is likely to come, firstly in the way that you view life, and secondly in the way you respond to life. But you should just allow meditation to change your life, rather than to change your life in order to meditate.

How Long?

The next question is, how long should each meditation session last? And how, if you are deep in meditation, do you know that your time is up?

The best advice for beginners is not to think too much about time. Keep in mind the idea of five minutes or so, and when the time is up you will automatically feel it is right to stop. It really doesn't matter

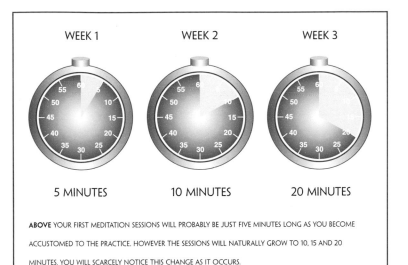

WEEK 1	WEEK 2	WEEK 3
5 MINUTES	10 MINUTES	20 MINUTES

ABOVE YOUR FIRST MEDITATION SESSIONS WILL PROBABLY BE JUST FIVE MINUTES LONG AS YOU BECOME ACCUSTOMED TO THE PRACTICE. HOWEVER THE SESSIONS WILL NATURALLY GROW TO 10, 15 AND 20 MINUTES. YOU WILL SCARCELY NOTICE THIS CHANGE AS IT OCCURS.

if you go over or under the five minutes at first. After a few days, you will find that your mind tunes in to this period of time, and knows when it is over. Do not be tempted to go on much longer than this, however successful your meditation seems to be. It is always best to take a gradual approach to meditation.

After you have been practising meditation for some little time (it may be days, it may be weeks, depending upon you) you will find a strange thing happens. Your period of five minutes begins to lengthen of its own accord. It still feels like five minutes, but when you look at your watch afterwards you will find that little by little it stretches into 10 minutes, then 15 minutes and so on. For time does funny things in meditation. In fact, you seem to lose your sense of time. Finally, you will find yourself sitting for 20 or 30 minutes each day, and this period will feel 'right' for you.

Naturally this won't happen if your mind is concentrating on time. Perhaps you are meditating in the morning and keep thinking of things you have to do during the day. If this is your problem, either get up a little earlier, or switch to meditating at night. Once you have reached the length of time that feels right for you, you can now start to discipline yourself by sitting for just that little bit longer. If 20 minutes feels right you can try sitting for 25 or if 30 seems right, you can try sitting for 40. *Don't push yourself too hard.* There are no prizes for sitting longer. but the extra time is a way of disciplining the mind, of making it that bit more concentrated.

If and when you do set yourself to sit a little longer than your normal period, you will need something to tell you when time is up. Set an alarm, but choose one with a sound that is soft and peaceful. This is better than stopping to peep at your watch. It's also better than relying on someone else to tell you.

Whichever method you choose to adopt, it's very important to sit for the amount of time you intend. Not only does this help to create the necessary discipline, it is often in these 'difficult' last few minutes, when we feel like giving up, that we gain most insight into ourselves.

LEFT SETTING AN ALARM CLOCK IS A GOOD WAY OF ENSURING THAT YOUR MEDITATION SESSION DOES NOT OVERRUN. DO BE CAREFUL IN YOUR CHOICE OF ALARM, HOWEVER.

WHERE TO SIT

If meditation is to become a regular part of your life, it is important that you should find your own 'right' place. Certainly you should be able to meditate anywhere, outdoors or indoors, and a time will come when you will be able to do so. But particularly in the early stages of your practice, a special place for your meditation is enormously helpful. Like a regular time of day, a particular place will turn your mind towards your practice. Your special place becomes linked in

ABOVE A SPECIAL PLACE FOR MEDITATION CAN HELP TO CREATE THE RIGHT ATMOSPHERE. REMEMBER TO UNPLUG THE TELEPHONE AND CHOOSE AN APPROPRIATE LIGHTING LEVEL. YOU MAY ALSO CHOOSE TO USE AN INCENSE BURNER.

29

your thoughts and your emotions with the inner peace you experience in your meditation. You may like to think of this special place as a place of power, where you become one with your surroundings and build up the energies you need to cope with life.

This place of power can be a corner of a bedroom or a living room or a small room devoted just to the purpose. In summer, it can be a place in the garden. It helps if you decorate this special place in some way – perhaps with pictures that have a special meaning for you, perhaps with a statue (rupa) of the Buddha, the prince of meditators. Or perhaps with a religious symbol such as the cross, or with a mandala or a yantra (see chapter 6).

LEFT A STATUE OF BUDDHA MAY HELP TO INSPIRE YOU IN YOUR MEDITATION. ALTERNATIVELY OTHER RELIGIOUS SYMBOLS MAY HAVE MORE MEANING FOR YOU.

You might like to consider constructing a small bench-like table, about half a metre by 15 centimetres (18 by 6 inches), and standing no more than 10 centimetres or so (4 inches) high. You can keep this with your meditation cushion (*see* chapter 3), and place it in front of you to support your rupa or your cross each time you sit. You can also use it to support an incense burner. Find which incense suits you best and burn a stick that will last roughly the length of your meditation. Set if far enough away so that you don't inhale the smoke directly. The fragrance of incense has a calming effect, and over a period of time your place of meditation and the clothes you wear to meditate will take on this fragrance.

CLOTHES FOR MEDITATION

Should you wear something special to meditate? Again, this is a matter of finding what is best for you. You certainly need to be comfortable during meditation, so tight clothes should be avoided. A special garment, whether it be a robe, a tracksuit, nightwear or your bare skin, provides you with another 'prop' which helps to turn your mind in the right direction. But if the idea of changing your clothes

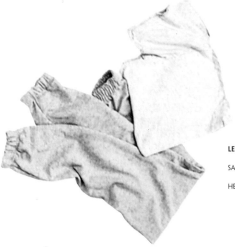

LEFT YOU MAY FIND THAT ALWAYS WEARING THE SAME COMFORTABLE CLOTHES WHEN MEDITATING HELPS TO PUT YOUR MIND IN THE RIGHT MOOD.

EXERCISE 2

Meditation involves the body as well as the mind, so it is useful to do a little work on the body to start off with. Sit quietly as in Exercise 1, and become aware of being 'me' once more. Just 'me', sitting here with 'myself'. Sit as still as you can. Now become aware of any discomfort you feel, and the urge to change position. This urge to move is a habit. Even though the discomfort is probably very slight, you feel the need to deal with it by moving.

Allow yourself to move. Now watch for discomfort again, and the urge once more to move. This time, sit through the urge. Notice that it is perfectly possible to resist it. Don't sit with it until you reach the point where you have a bad pain, but do be aware of how the restlessness of your mind is mirrored in physical movement. As soon as the mind encounters anything it thinks it dislikes, it urges you to act in order to remove it. It is this urge and the restlessness that it brings which sets up tensions. Gently allow yourself to sit through this urge. Stay still. Notice how stilling the body helps you to still the mind.

in order to meditate is too much of an effort, then forget about it, at least until your practice is well established. The most important thing is always the meditation itself, and you should avoid anything that might put you off doing it regularly.

In addition to wearing something comfortable, you also need to keep warm in order that cold does not distract you from your meditation. Once again, when your practice is well established, you will be able to meditate in near-freezing conditions without noticing it, but in the early stages don't subject yourself to extremes.

Now that you have established a time and a place for your meditation, it is a good idea to look at the body that you will be taking this journey in.

MEDITATION POSITIONS

CHAPTER THREE

Exercise 2 helped you recognize that the human body isn't comfortable in any one position for any length of time. Yet in meditation it is important to sit in stillness. The mind cannot become calm and still if the body is constantly fidgeting about.

But if you are to sit still, you have to find a position in which your body feels the minimum discomfort. The secret of such a position is balance. If the body is properly balanced, then it can learn, with a little patience, to remain as it is for at least an hour at a time.

THE LOTUS POSITION

In meditation, you should allow the body to achieve its natural state of balance. The lotus position is ideal for this. It provides the body with a firm base – the triangle formed by the buttocks and the crossed legs with knees touching the ground – and allows the spine, shoulders, neck and head to rest

LEFT THE BODY NEEDS TO BE IN A STATE OF PERFECT BALANCE IN ORDER FOR MEDITATION TO BE SUCCESSFUL.

comfortably on this base. But unless you use the lotus position from childhood, when you are at your most supple, you won't find it comes easily. How ever, if you have your buttocks 10 centimetres (4 inches) or so higher than your crossed legs (hence the need for the kind of cushion I describe in a moment) you can bring your knees nearer the floor, and this throws the weight of the body forward, making it much easier to keep a straight back. In the full-lotus position, the legs are then crossed, the right foot placed on the left thigh and the left foot placed on the right.

ABOVE IN THE FULL-LOTUS POSITION, BOTH FEET ARE PLACED ON THE THIGHS AND THE BACK IS STRAIGHT.

33

THE HALF-LOTUS POSITION

You may prefer to settle for the half-lotus, in which one foot (right or left) is placed on the opposite thigh, while the other foot remains on the floor with the heel as close as possible to the perineum (the space between the genitals and anus).

THE PERFECT OR MAGICIAN'S POSITION

For most Westerners, even the half-lotus is difficult. You may therefore choose the 'perfect' or 'magician's' posture. In this posture, the uppermost foot rests on the calf. This position has most of the benefits of the full-lotus, feels better balanced than the half-lotus, and comes to most people after a relatively short period of practice.

USING THE PERFECT
OR MAGICIAN'S POSTURE

Make or buy a meditation cushion (a round or square one, 30 centimetres (1 foot) or so in diameter), hard enough to support you 10 centimetres (4 inches) from the floor. Now sit on the cushion, with your legs straight in front of you. Bend your left leg, take the foot in your hands and draw it up against the body so that the heel rests against the perineum. Now edge the buttocks forward a little on your cushion, so the perineum rests almost on top of the heel. Then take the right leg and cross it over the left, bringing the foot up so that it rests on the calf or nestles into the groove between calf and thigh. Your knees should now be flat on the floor, and the whole body poised and at ease.

You can reverse the position of the legs if you like, so that the left is on top of the right (and indeed it's a good thing to be able to achieve the position either way around, so that your two legs become equally supple), but remember always to draw the lower heel in as close to the body as possible, and then slide forward on your cushion until you are almost sitting on it.

At first, you will probably find that once you're in the required position it feels extremely uncomfortable. Your upper foot will probably hurt from being lifted up on to the calf of the lower leg, and your knees will stick awkwardly into the air instead of resting flat on the floor. Don't worry. And don't try to force yourself into the position. You can try edging a little further forward on your cushion, or raising the cushion another couple of centimetres, but the important thing is to remind yourself that each day the position will become easier. Before long, you will be able to hold it without difficulty.

Some meditation teachers, particularly those trained in the hatha yoga tradition, suggest you should push down gently on the knees with your hands, encouraging them to rest on the floor. But a better suggestion is to relax the legs as much as you can, and then allow the leg muscles to press the knees down throughout the meditation period. Before too long you will find you can obtain the correct position without much trouble.

35

ABOVE MANY WESTERNERS FIND THE LOTUS AND HALF-
LOTUS POSITIONS UNCOMFORTABLE AND PREFER TO
MEDITATE IN THE PERFECT POSTURE, IN WHICH ONE FOOT IS
PLACED ON THE CALF OF THE OTHER,

THE MODIFIED 'PERFECT' POSITION

If, in spite of everything, you still find it almost impossible to bring one foot up on to the opposite calf, keep it on the floor and, provided your knees are in the right position, simply draw it up close against the calf into the modified 'perfect' position.

ABOVE THE MODIFIED 'PERFECT' POSITION IS A GOOD ALTERNATIVE TO THE LOTUS IF YOU CANNOT BRING YOUR FEET ONTO YOUR CALVES.

THE CROSS-LEGGED POSITION

If none of these positions work for you, then just sit cross-legged. But be warned – for the body to be comfortable, the knees must be lower than the buttocks. If they aren't, your weight is thrown backwards, and you will react by leaning the upper body forward. The result is discomfort, backache, and a feeling that meditation isn't what it's cracked up to be.

Since the knees are high when you sit cross-legged, you'll need a cushion or support that will lift and keep your buttocks 20 centimetres (8 inches) or so off the floor if you want to use this position.

USING A MEDITATION STOOL

There are alternatives to the positions I've just described. One is to buy or make a meditation stool.

The simplest stool is rather like the meditation table I described in the last chapter, a bench-type object with a seat of 30 centimetres (1 foot) long by 15 centimetres (6 inches) wide, and resting on two stout supports which run from front to back. The seat should slope forwards. The best angle for this slope is to have the front edge of the seat three-quarters the height of the rear edge. Some experimentation is needed in order to find how high the stool itself needs to be, since long-legged people will inevitably want it higher than short. The important thing, however, is that your legs need to be tucked comfortably underneath it, so that you are in effect kneeling on the floor, yet with the buttocks supported by the stool instead of resting on the heels.

USING A CHAIR

If you're unhappy with this position too, sit in a chair – provided it's upright and you can sit in it with the lower back straight.

Not only is slouching bad for the back and highly uncomfortable, it also prompts the mind to slouch too. Make sure the chair is a firm one, and that it is at a height that allows you to place your feet flat on the floor. But unless you have a disability which makes it difficult for you to sit on a cushion or on a meditation stool, it's better not to rely on a chair.

The very act of getting into a special meditation position is another of the props that help settle your mind into the right state.

POSITIONING THE

RIGHT AS A LAST RESORT, YOU COULD CHOOSE TO
SIT IN A CHAIR DURING MEDITATION. IT MUST HAVE
A HARD SEAT AND A STRAIGHT BACK.

MORE ABOUT POSTURE

It is a sad fact that our posture is at its best in the early years of life, and from then on gets progressively worse. Watch a small baby, just old enough to sit up unsupported. Notice the straightness of the back – no curve, no slump. Watch an older child running or walking. Notice how the head, is held erect, how the spine is supple and how graceful the movements are. Now look at the adolescent – the hunched shoulders, the droop of the back, the head thrust forward, the shambling walk.

Now watch someone who is feeling down and see how this is mirrored in their body. Compare them with someone in high spirits, and see how different their posture is. The close links between mind and body are especially noticeable in posture. If you feel dejected, notice how your feelings change if you straighten up, and look ahead rather than down at the ground. Finally, see how much easier it is to stay awake if you sit in an upright chair than if you slump down on a sofa.

Once you are aware of these facts, it isn't hard to understand why posture is so important in meditation. One day, as an advanced meditator, you will be able to meditate lying flat on your back in your bed if you wish. But until that time arrives, a straight back, and an upright though relaxed posture, are the rules of the day.

LEFT AS WE PROGRESS THROUGH LIFE, OUR POSTURE TENDS TO DETERIORATE. YOU WILL FIND THEREFORE THAT YOU HAVE TO MAKE A SPECIAL EFFORT TO KEEP YOUR BACK STRAIGHT AT FIRST.

38

POSITIONING THE HANDS

The final point about posture is the hands. You may notice when looking at pictures of meditators that they hold their hands in a number of different ways:

some have their hand palms downwards on their knees

some have their palms upwards, perhaps with the thumbs and first fingers touching

some have the hands resting in the lap with the fingers entwined in various different ways, known sometimes as 'mudras'

At this early part of your meditation journey, the important thing is to keep the hands relaxed and comfortable, so that they do not distract you from what you are doing. They can either lie on the knees or in the lap, as you prefer. If you would like to make use of a mudra, the most common one is the 'O' shape, as discussed in chapter 6.

39

If your hands are lying palm upwards on your knees, form this circle by placing the thumb and forefinger of each hand lightly together. If your fingers are interlaced in your lap, place the two thumbs together and raise them slightly so that there is a circle shape above the fingers. Or separate the fingers and allow the palm of one hand to rest on top of the other, while again bringing the thumbs together and lifting them slightly to form this circle shape.

RIGHT A HAND POSITION CAN BE ANOTHER PROP TO HELP YOU IN YOUR MEDITATION. CHOOSE A POSITION THAT YOU ARE COMFORTABLE WITH, AS YOU DO NOT WANT IT TO BECOME A DISTRACTION.

EXERCISE 3

Now that you have found the right posture for your meditation,
your body will adapt to it more readily if you practise that posture
during the day even when you're not actually meditating. Take up
the position while watching television for example, or while
listening to music or the radio.

However, when carrying out this exercise, don't hold the position
until it becomes a strain. If your muscles become stiff, you will
have to stop practising for a few days until the stiffness wears off.
Also, remember to stay relaxed while in the posture. If your legs
seem especially reluctant to cross themselves in the way you want,
this is probably because you are too tense. Relax into the posture,
rather than force yourself into it.

Experiment a little at first with your hand positions, but once you
have found what suits you, don't keep chopping and changing. It's
better to be consistent, as this helps to keep the mind clear.

MEDITATION IN EVERYDAY LIFE

One final word. When meditation becomes a part of your life, you
need to be able to enter the state whenever you wish – travelling on
a train, waiting for a bus, preparing to go into a meeting, sitting by a
river, lying in bed, even walking down a busy street.

Some of these forms of meditation are very similar to your usual sitting meditation practice. Others of them, such as walking meditation, involve a special kind of alertness to your surroundings (*see* chapter 6). These practices should be carried out in addition to, rather than instead of your usual daily practice. But they do show that meditation, although it is often helped by it, should not depend entirely upon any one special physical position.

Remember that meditation is something that you carry with you in your mind, not something that you get from the outside world. It is your own possession – the experience of who you are, now, in each moment.

THE WAYS AND MEANS

CHAPTER FOUR

You have already started on your meditation journey. The decision to meditate is your first step, and the act of sitting down in the right place and in the right posture is the second. You're now ready to take the third step.

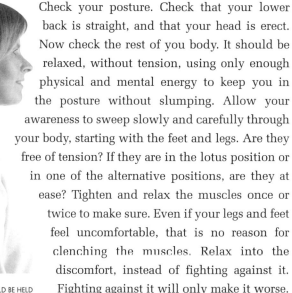

Check your posture. Check that your lower back is straight, and that your head is erect. Now check the rest of you body. It should be relaxed, without tension, using only enough physical and mental energy to keep you in the posture without slumping. Allow your awareness to sweep slowly and carefully through your body, starting with the feet and legs. Are they free of tension? If they are in the lotus position or in one of the alternative positions, are they at ease? Tighten and relax the muscles once or twice to make sure. Even if your legs and feet feel uncomfortable, that is no reason for clenching the muscles. Relax into the discomfort, instead of fighting against it. Fighting against it will only make it worse. Now check the buttocks, and next the abdomen. Let go of any stress that you feel

ABOVE YOUR NECK SHOULD BE HELD ERECT, BUT THERE SHOULD BE NO TENSION IN THE JOINTS.

there. Proceed upwards to the back, the chest, the arms and hands, the shoulders, the neck, and finally the jaw, the face and the temples.

Be aware of what is going on in your own body. Tension is simply the body preparing for action. If the action is not performed, we all too often leave the tension locked up in the muscles instead of releasing it. As your awareness sweeps your body, think of gently releasing this tension, and allowing the energy to flow naturally back into the rest of the body.

One-pointed Attention

So now you are relaxed, sitting expectantly on your seat. What happens next? The answer is simple. You concentrate. Concentration is the still point at the centre of meditation. Whatever system you use, it revolves around this centre. Meditation is impossible without concentration. A deep inner concentration, unhurried, without anxiety, without tension. It is like the quiet watchfulness with which someone observes a bird from close at hand, knowing that the slightest movement will startle it into flight.

What Does Attention Mean?

There is a revealing story about a young monk who comes to ask the Zen master Ikkyo for some wise words to help him live his life. Ikkyo answers him by writing down the single pictogram for 'attention'. The young monk is puzzled, and asks Ikkyo for something more. Ikkyo agrees and writes down 'attention', 'attention', 'attention'. The young monk is even more puzzled, and asks Ikkyo what does 'attention, attention, attention', mean? Ikkyo writes down 'attention, attention, attention means attention'.

LEFT IF THE MIND STAYS IN ONE PLACE, THE MEDITATOR CAN OBSERVE THOUGHTS PASSING AWAY, LIKE CLOUDS CROSSING THE FACE OF THE SKY.

If you prefer, you can use the word 'attention' rather than concentration. 'Attention' suggests the lightness and relaxation that you should feel during meditation. There is nothing fierce about this attention. You should be focused and clear, but you should achieve this through gentleness rather than effort, by the simple decision to observe rather than by teeth-gritting determination to do so. You attend because your are attending, not because you are striving to do so.

So in meditation you attend. In that attention, the mind becomes centred instead of distracted by thoughts or sensations. The mind remains in one place, instead of chasing off madly after different thoughts. These may continue to arise, but if the mind stays in one place the meditator is able to observe them arising and then passing away, like clouds crossing the face of the sky, rather than allowing them to take over.

A helpful name for this attention is one-pointed attention. The mind remains focused on one thing, on one point, and refuses to be distracted from it. It refuses to turn aside and become lost in the thoughts and sensations that arise. It refuses to judge them, it even refuses to banish them. It just lets them be. The mind remains simply in a state of awareness in which it experiences itself rather than the thoughts that crowd into it.

THE MEANS OF TRANSPORT

If you are to attend in this way, what should you be attending to? Or, to return to the idea of a journey, if you are to travel, what is to be your means of transport? You can travel on – fix your awareness on –

sound, vision, words, inner pictures, a candle flame, a string of meditation beads, on virtually anything on which the mind can settle and stay settled. Each of these has its advantages, and I have more to say about them in chapter 6. One of the most valuable ways of travelling is on the breath. And there are good reasons for this.

REASONS FOR TRAVELLING ON THE BREATH

- **The breath is always with you.**
- **The breath is rhythmical and balanced – a steady coming and going – and this rhythm and balance helps collect and steady the mind.**
- **The breath is a symbol of the life-force. It symbolizes the mystery of being alive.**
- **The breath has about it that lightness that is so important in meditation. As you relax in meditation so the breath, like the mind, slows down, becomes calmer, softer, less noticeable, until finally it becomes just a whisper.**

45

So the breath is an ideal aid with which to travel. Even if you decide later to focus your attention on another object of meditation, your early training in watching your breath will be invaluable to you. It will prepare you for these other forms of meditation. Also, you will find that in each meditation session, a few opening minutes spent watching the breath before you turn your attention elsewhere are ideal for putting the mind into the correct state.

RIGHT FIX YOUR AWARENESS ON A CANDLE FLAME, OR VIRTUALLY ANYTHING ON WHICH THE MIND CAN SETTLE.

USING THE BREATH

Having settled yourself into your meditation position and decided to focus on the breathing, what do you do next? Let's go through it step by step.

LOWER YOUR EYELIDS

There are open-eye and closed-eye meditations, and there are meditations done with the eyes half shut. Each has its purpose (*see* chapter 6). But for the method you are going to try, either close your eyes completely or bring them so nearly closed that you can only see a slit of light. Either way is acceptable, though you many find that keeping the eyes slightly open helps prevent you from feeling drowsy. But make sure your eyelids stay relaxed. There should be no effort, no tension involved in keeping them in this slightly open position.

ABOVE CLOSE YOUR EYES, OR KEEP THEM NEARLY CLOSED, BUT ENSURE THAT YOUR EYELIDS ARE RELAXED.

TURN YOUR ATTENTION TO YOUR BREATHING

At first, just be aware of your breathing. Notice how the breath flows in and out effortlessly, almost as if you are being breathed rather than breathing. Notice how it feels cool as you breathe in, and warm as you breathe out. Notice how the body rises and falls with each in-breath and each out-breath. Now turn your attention to where the breath is going. Is it going into your upper chest? Your middle chest? Or is it flowing deep down into your abdomen? The last of these is the correct place. In meditation, you breathe deeply, but deep breathing does not mean taking enormous gulps of air. It means drawing the breath down into the body as deeply as possible,

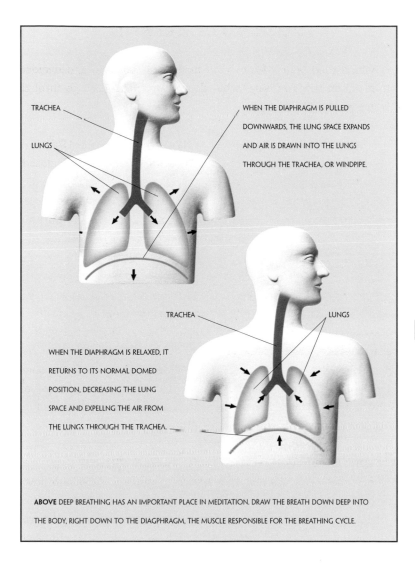

TRACHEA

LUNGS

WHEN THE DIAPHRAGM IS PULLED
DOWNWARDS, THE LUNG SPACE EXPANDS
AND AIR IS DRAWN INTO THE LUNGS
THROUGH THE TRACHEA, OR WINDPIPE.

TRACHEA

LUNGS

WHEN THE DIAPHRAGM IS RELAXED, IT
RETURNS TO ITS NORMAL DOMED
POSITION, DECREASING THE LUNG
SPACE AND EXPELLNG THE AIR FROM
THE LUNGS THROUGH THE TRACHEA.

ABOVE DEEP BREATHING HAS AN IMPORTANT PLACE IN MEDITATION. DRAW THE BREATH DOWN DEEP INTO
THE BODY, RIGHT DOWN TO THE DIAGPHRAGM, THE MUSCLE RESPONSIBLE FOR THE BREATHING CYCLE.

right down to the diaphragm, the biggest muscle in the body, and
the one responsible for making you breathe. Practise this for a
moment, but without making any effort to take in more air than
usual. Natural, relaxed breathing is your aim. If you begin to feel
light-headed, pause for a moment.

DECIDE ON A POINT OF ATTENTION

Now decide where it feels natural to place your concentration during this awareness of your breathing. Is it at the nostrils, where you feel the sensation of the cool air flowing in and the warm air flowing out? Or is it at the abdomen, where you feel the gentle rise and fall of each breath? Both places are taught in different meditation systems. The nostrils have an advantage in that the changes there are smaller and so require closer attention. The nostrils are also the point at which air enters the body, so they are the point of contact between the life-force inside us and the life-forces outside us. But the abdomen allows us to become more aware of our bodies, and helps us to feel more in contact with ourselves. Experiment with both points of concentration if you like, but having decided on one, keep to it. Above all, never be tempted to switch from one point to another during a meditation session. Decide where the attention is going to be focused at the beginning of the session, and keep it there.

48

COUNT YOUR BREATHS

Particularly in the early stages of your training in meditation, you are likely to find that you need to use other methods in order to help you concentrate. Counting your in-breaths and out-breaths can be most effective. Count each out-breath, from one to ten, then go back to one

---

THE BUDDHA AND BREATHING

The Buddha himself taught breathing as a way to assist meditation:

Mindfully he breathes in, mindfully he breathes out. Breathing out a long breath he knows 'I breathe out a long breath'; breathing in a long breath he knows 'I breathe in a long breath'. Breathing out a short breath he knows 'I breathe out a short breath'; breathing in a short breath, he knows 'I breathe in a short breath'.

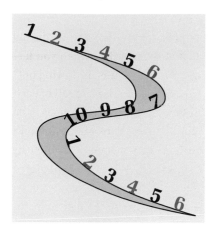

and start again. If at any point your attention wanders and you lose count, go back to one. Once you find you are able to meditate for 15 minutes without losing the count you can give up counting, but be prepared to use it again if ever your mind is particularly active and meditation becomes difficult.

ABOVE 'MINDFULLY HE BREATHES IN,
MINDFULLY HE BREATHES OUT'.

Now begin. And watch what happens.

LAPSES OF ATTENTION

At first, even with the aid of counting your breaths, you may find that the mind soon wanders away. Thoughts arise, capture your attention, and before you realize what's happening, your counting, your awareness of breathing, and the whole idea of meditation itself has faded from view.

Don't worry.
Don't be impatient.
Don't be angry or disgusted or frustrated with yourself.

These lapses of attention happen to us all. But the more annoyed we become about it, the harder things get.

Remember that it is because your mind is so scattered and out of control that you need to meditate. If your mind wasn't like this, your whole life would already be a meditation, and there would be no need to find a special time and place in which to sit and practise.

PROBLEM-SOLVING AND
CREATIVITY IN MEDITATION

Once you begin to develop the ability to concentrate upon the breathing, is it possible to concentrate instead upon a problem, and allow the mind to come up with a solution? And if meditation is supposed to help creativity, how does this work?

PROBLEM-SOLVING

Many people find that meditation helps them to solve problems. But this isn't done by focusing on the problem instead of upon the breathing. Most of us have had the experience of going to sleep with a problem at the back of our minds, and finding the solution there in the morning. What happens is that the unconscious mind (the part responsible for our dreams) goes on working during sleep and, freed from the interference of the conscious mind, is sometimes able to find the necessary solution.

Something similar can happen in meditation. Although the conscious mind does not fall asleep, it does quieten down. This allows us to listen to the unconscious mind. The difference is that while we're awake we're usually too busy to listen to it. In meditation, we begin to listen. We don't have to tell our mind to work on the problem. It is already aware of the need. We put the problem on one side, and as we come out of the meditation, we may find the solution to it comes at the same time.

CREATIVITY

Creativity also depends upon the unconscious.

Before starting to write or paint you may find it helpful to meditate for a few minutes. This can even be done while sitting at your desk. Sit upright, close your eyes, and focus on your breathing. Don't think about your work. Allow the mind to open out and become clear. Then open your eyes and get on with the job. Notice how ideas now come to you more readily.

Sometimes solutions to problems (and creative ideas) come to you during the meditation, and you may fear that these ideas will be lost unless you get up straight away and write them down. Don't worry. Note them in passing, just like any other thoughts, but mark them so that you can call on them once the meditation is over. With a little practice, you will find that they come back readily enough.

51

In the East, one of the symbols for the mind is a chattering monkey. Each moment of our waking lives this monkey tries to distract us from what we are doing, muddling and confusing us, making us forget what happened even five minutes ago, taking our attention away from life instead of allowing us to get on with the business of living it.

You rediscover this fact each time you sit in meditation. Welcome this rediscovery. It reminds you that you are on a journey that we should all undertake if we value ourselves enough to want to find out who we are and make better use of ourselves. And each time you make this discovery, bring your mind gently back to its point of focus. If it happens ten times, if it happens a hundred times the remedy is always the same. Gently but firmly return your concentration to your breathing.

Discovering the Mind

After a while, perhaps during this first meditation, perhaps during the second, perhaps during the 102nd, you will find that the mind enters a state of one-pointedness, a state in which your whole attention is focused upon your breathing and your counting. For a moment, thoughts fade into the background and may even cease to arise altogether. The mind is simply there, doing nothing and being nothing other than itself. This is your first moment of discovery that you, the real you, the essential you, exists separately from your thoughts. You are not your thoughts. Descartes' famous dictum 'I think therefore I am', is seen at that moment to be absurdly false. It should be turned around to read 'I am, therefore I think'.

The significance of this moment, when thoughts stop but you continue to exist, will only strike you when the moment has passed, for the simple reason that the act of realizing this significance is itself a thought. Even the realization that you have stopped thinking is a thought, and once you have a thought, then the moment is gone.

When you look back upon this after the meditation is over, you will make a second strange discovery. You will realize that you can only experience this 'thought-less' state as a unity (something made up of one part), not as a duality (made up of two parts). That is, you can't be in it and aware that you are in it at the same time. You can't split your mind into two parts. You can only be whole, nothing less.

This and the various other insights that come to you in meditation are there when you are not looking directly at them, and gone the moment you are. They do not allow a separation between you and your awareness. There is no separation between what is being done and the person doing it. And therefore (though this may be difficult to understand until you have experienced it) there is nothing being done and nobody doing it. There is only a moment of completeness.

One of the best known of all koans, those strange riddles used in Zen which appear to have no solution and which push the mind beyond rational thought, emphasizes this completeness by asking:

'What is the sound of one hand clapping?'

How absurd. Clapping by definition is the act of two hands, so how can one hand clap? How indeed. And yet in meditation one hand claps. Or does it? The use of koans in meditation is fully discussed in chapter 6, where we shall see that it is the strength of a person's concentration and not the power of the intellect that determines his or her progress.

THE PROBLEM WITH WORDS

But these are, of course, just words. And valuable as words are, there is a danger that they can get in the way. So when I start talking about 'unity' and 'duality' and 'no separation, nothing being done and nobody doing it', I may be confusing you or setting up a 'goal' which you now feel you should try and reach.

Often individuals, when they are beginning the practice of meditation, ask if they are doing it 'right'. I implied in chapter 1 that the journey of meditation leads to a destination that can only be known once one has arrived (when in fact the whole idea of 'destination' and 'arriving' may change their meaning). So don't let me mislead you through words into thinking that I am describing a state which is 'right'. I am simply trying to put into words something that cannot be explained by words.

There is a big difference (as poets tell us) between direct experience and our descriptions of that experience. If my words succeed, then you understand them at a wordless level. If they fail, do not make the mistake of seeing in them something that is not there.

POETRY AND MEDITATION

In the same way that the words in this book are trying to put across the essence of the experience of meditation rather than what it really is, so poetry tries to put across the the feeling of an experience rather than a literal account of it.

Japanese haiku (short verses usually presented in English in just three or four lines) are a particularly good example of poets trying to encapsulate the sensation of an experience, allowing us to identify with them at a level beyond the 'nowness' of experience, allowing us to live it through the poet as if he or she is recalling memories of our own past.

Take for example a haiku such as:

> Snow capped as they are,
> The gentle slopes of the mountains
> Fade into the hazy mist
> At twilight on a spring day.

Written nearly five centuries ago by Sogi as the first verse of a longer poem, these four simple lines speak to us as if it were we ourselves who stand watching the outlines of the mountains fade into the soft evening mist. For a timeless moment, we are Sogi and he is us. The boundaries between us have dissolved as the outlines of the mountains dissolve. With a few exquisite touches of his poet's brush, Sogi tells us all we need to know about the mountains and all we need to know about his feelings for them. Like all haiku poets, he identifies the qualities in an experience that prompted a reaction in him and gives them to us so that we can make of them what we will.

ARCHERY AND MEDITATION

The German philosopher and Zen student Eugene Herrigel studied archery under the Zen master Kenzo Awa. In the form in which Herrigel studied it, archery, like the other martial arts, is itself a form of meditation, a meticulous exercise in total relaxed concentration. In the course of his long, often frustrating but richly rewarding apprenticeship with Kenzo Awa, Herrigel learns that Zen archery consists in:

'...the archer aiming at himself yet not at himself, in hitting himself – yet not himself, and thus becoming simultaneously the aimer and the aim, the hitter or the hit. Or... to become in spite of himself an unmoved centre. Then comes the supreme and ultimate miracle; art becomes artless, shooting becomes not-shooting, a shooting without bow and arrow; the teacher becomes a pupil again, the Master a beginner, the end a beginning, and the beginning perfection.'

This is an example of one-pointed concentration. In the same way that Herrigel experienced this during archery, you can learn to experience it through meditation.

EXERCISE 4

All this may sound confusingly mystical. You may look back at the benefits listed in Box 1 (in chapter 1) and ask what has happened to these. Talk of a 'thought-less' mind and of unity may be all very well, but what about the more down-to-earth benefits like increased patience and better sleep and lower blood pressure?

Many of these will happen in their own time. Don't be impatient for them. Allow them to arise almost incidentally. Do, however, try to use some of your new ability for concentration and self-awareness. When carrying out a task of some kind, when listening to someone talking to you, when reading, use some of the attention you use in meditation. Try to be there in the moment, just as you are there in the moment during meditation. Don't let your attention wander off.

If you have trouble sleeping, focus upon your breathing when you get to bed, but this time with the idea not of staying alert as in meditation but of sinking down into sleep with each breath. It's usually the busy chatter of the mind that keeps us awake. By focusing attention on the breathing instead of on thoughts, the mind is free to do what nature intends and drift into slumber.

Finally, keep a meditator's diary. Don't be slavish about it. Write brief entries giving descriptions of your meditation. Do not try to evaluate your experiences. ('Mind particularly active; kept returning to thoughts of busy day ahead tomorrow', rather than 'Bad meditation; mind just wouldn't stop chattering'.) Note as well any changes in your everyday behaviour. Extra patience with a trying colleague for example. New-found calmness in crisis. More optimism and feelings of happiness. Don't go looking for progress. Simply note it as it occurs. Be prepared for it to be excellent one day, and to be back where you started from the next. Note it, and go on with your practice.

If you wish, you could also record in your diary any particular insights that you have during or as a result of meditation. But don't make too much of them. As on any journey, the scenery is changing all the time. Early insights may be replaced by later ones, so see each one as temporary. Don't become too attached to them or they could get in the way of future progress.

BELOW USE A DIARY TO RECORD ANY PARTICULAR INSIGHTS THAT YOU HAVE DURING, OR AS A RESULT OF, MEDITATION.

57

PROBLEMS ONCE ONE-POINTED ATTENTION IS ACHIEVED

When you do achieve one-pointed attention, do not make the mistake of attaching importance to it. If you do, if you start judging it, not only do you lose it for that meditation session, you may lose it for many sessions to come.

What happens is that the mind, having decided that this experience is a 'good thing', now tries to take over and re-create it. But this is exactly what you must not do. Because the mind will now try consciously, deliberately, to produce this moment of one-pointed concentration for you. And the harder it tries, the more certain it is to fail. The mind has fallen into the trap of thinking that it can 'will' this state. But this of course is impossible, because as long as there is a mind trying to achieve this state and a state waiting to be achieved, you cannot experience that wholeness, that unity, which is what the state – in the limited way in which we can describe it – actually is.

And there is another danger. Namely that having entered this state, however briefly, you may decide afterwards it was rather disappointing. How ordinary! You had been expecting deep mystical revelations, sensations of indescribable bliss, long moments where you entered the heart of the universe and witnessed its secrets. A fleeting experience of just being present in your own awareness isn't what you're after at all.

Wait. You are still only at the beginning of your journey. You are again, from a different angle, trying to judge your own experience and give it marks out of ten. You should neither be excited nor disappointed by what you have seen. This is the state of mind that lies at the centre of all states of mind, but because you have received a whisper of it does not mean that you have listened to the whole story.

To return to the idea of a journey, you have seen something from the train window, but you do not yet know what it is you have seen. Only time will tell what it was that you saw. If 'tell' is the word for it.

FOLLOWING THE PATH

CHAPTER FIVE

THE VALUE OF PATIENCE

O ne of the most important things to take with you on your meditation journey is patience. The patience to sit. The patience not to become frustrated with yourself when your attention constantly strays from your breathing and wanders off after your thoughts. The patience not to expect too much too soon. The patience indeed not to 'expect' anything.

'But I don't have that kind of patience' you may be saying. 'I'm not the sort of person who can sit and wait for results. I like to get on with things, and I like to know where I'm going.' However, the very fact of your impatience is a sure sign that you need to meditate. Meditation develops patience, but patience of a very special kind. This is the sort of patience that

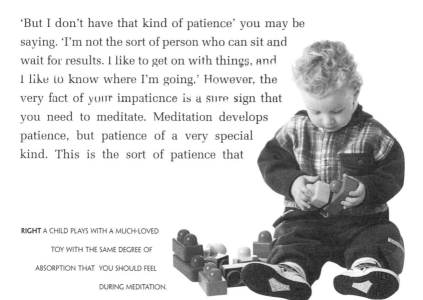

RIGHT A CHILD PLAYS WITH A MUCH-LOVED TOY WITH THE SAME DEGREE OF ABSORPTION THAT YOU SHOULD FEEL DURING MEDITATION.

comes from the realization that impatience makes us rush through life, always seeking the next experience and the next experience and the next experience, and missing the quality of every one of them.

In a way, you can say that the patience that develops with meditation is simply the awareness of the magic in each moment of life. Instead of patience, you could call it an absorbing interest. As I said in chapter 3, don't set yourself extravagant targets of how long you are going to sit. Begin with only five minutes. If you feel your patience won't last this long, begin with four. We all have some patience, however little. Use what you have. Begin at the beginning. Don't ask the impossible of yourself. Begin – and let meditation help take you forward from there.

PATIENT, STEADY PROGRESS

Exercise your patience in another way too. Many books on meditation present you with a huge range of meditation techniques. The temptation is to try them all. This only emphasizes once again our tendency to rush from one thing to another, dropping each before it has been properly tasted. In the great meditation traditions of both the Eastern and Western worlds, pupils remained with the single technique given to them by their teacher, often for years, until he or she felt it was time to give them another one. The problem in our modern world, where information is so freely available, is that we want to see everything and try everything straightaway. We want to know it all before we even know what it is we want to know.

So exercise patience by not trying to move too quickly from watching your breath to the other techniques described later in this book. Let me emphasize once again that attention is the key in all meditation, no matter what technique it is you are using. Attending to your breathing isn't the first lesson, from which we quickly graduate to higher things. It is the lesson that underlies all lessons, the first lesson and the last lesson and the 'essence' of all meditational practices.

STAGES ON THE JOURNEY

We now come to that point on the journey where we are able to see more of the countryside through which we are passing. We are able to see that meditation involves three stages which need to be taken one at a time and in a particular order. And yet, at the same time, these three stages also exist side by side. We do not leave stage one when entering stage two, or leave stage two when we enter stage three. As you explore the three stages you will see that they are one, and that although there are differences between them, there are no differences at all.

You have already started on the first stage, namely the development of concentration, of one-pointed attention. The next two stages are:

- *Tranquillity*
- *Insight*

61

LEFT CONCENTRATION HAS TO BE ACHIEVED BEFORE WE CAN MOVE ON TO THE STAGES OF TRANQUILLITY AND INSIGHT.

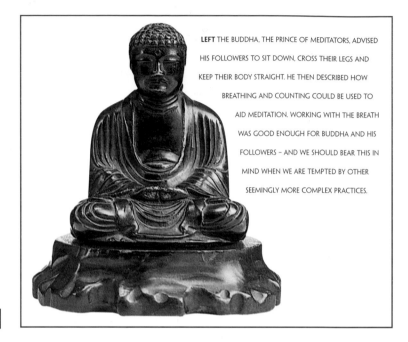

LEFT THE BUDDHA, THE PRINCE OF MEDITATORS, ADVISED HIS FOLLOWERS TO SIT DOWN, CROSS THEIR LEGS AND KEEP THEIR BODY STRAIGHT. HE THEN DESCRIBED HOW BREATHING AND COUNTING COULD BE USED TO AID MEDITATION. WORKING WITH THE BREATH WAS GOOD ENOUGH FOR BUDDHA AND HIS FOLLOWERS – AND WE SHOULD BEAR THIS IN MIND WHEN WE ARE TEMPTED BY OTHER SEEMINGLY MORE COMPLEX PRACTICES.

Until we have achieved concentration we cannot achieve tranquillity, and until we have achieved tranquillity we cannot achieve insight. And yet insight is really only insight into tranquillity, while tranquillity is only the calm state in which insight appears. Two views through the same window, two windows through which to see the same view. And neither of them can be achieved without concentration, since tranquillity and insight are what happens when the mind is totally absorbed in concentration.

RIGHT WE RARELY GIVE OUR FULL ATTENTION TO SOMEONE WHEN WE ARE LISTENING TO THEM. BY FOCUSING ON WHAT THEY ARE ACTUALLY SAYING WE CAN BEGIN TO DEVELOP OUR POWERS OF CONCENTRATION.

EXERCISE 5

You can of course help yourself develop concentration by practising a few simple exercises which can be done during normal daily life. Here are some examples:

- Listen more carefully when other people talk. Instead of allowing the mind to busy itself with what you are going to say next, actually focus upon listening. Don't be distracted by random thoughts about the person who is talking, keep the attention focused upon the words and their meaning.
- Take an object (for example, an ornament, a flower, a picture) and really study it for a few minutes. Don't become distracted by thoughts about it or by reactions to it. Just look at the object, allowing your eyes to move slowly over it, studying it from every angle. Experience it, don't think about it.

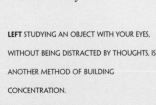

- Run your hand over an uneven surface, for example the clothes you are wearing. Concentrate on the feel of the material, the varying textures of wool and cotton, the roughness and the smoothness, the raised contours of creases and pleats. Don't label the sensation, just experience it. Listen to the variations in the sound made by your hand as it moves over the material. Don't think what the sounds are 'like'. Hear them as they are.

LEFT STUDYING AN OBJECT WITH YOUR EYES, WITHOUT BEING DISTRACTED BY THOUGHTS, IS ANOTHER METHOD OF BUILDING CONCENTRATION.

I return in chapter 6 to the question of concentrating more upon the things around you instead of being lost in thought, but try to use your developing concentration more in ordinary life. Begin really to look at and to hear the world, instead of passing it by, lost in inner thoughts.

TRANQUILLITY

What exactly does tranquillity mean?

Take the image of a pond, and imagine stirring up the muddy bottom with a stick. Watch as the mud rises, clouding the water so that you can no longer see into the depths. Now put the stick to one side and watch as the mud settles. Watch the water, little by little, becoming clear again, until you can once more see into its centre. Notice how still the water becomes. Nothing moves. The water is so clear that you can't even be sure there is water there until you reach down and bathe your fingers in it.

Tranquillity is like the clearness of the water. It is that state of mind in which nothing stirs up the mud of our restless thoughts or emotions.

There is, however, nothing passive or stagnant about tranquillity. To understand this, imagine the water overflowing at one end of the pond. Imagine it overflowing gently, but gathering pace and cascading down the mountainside. In spite of its movement, the water remains as clear as when it was in the pond.

Remember that it is the clearness which is tranquillity, not the stillness or the movement. The clearness or tranquillity of your mind can exist in both stillness and movement, but without it, insight is impossible. How can you see into the heart of things unless what you are looking through is clear?

Some people ask if tranquillity is the same thing as relaxation. Of course it is, in the sense that when you are tranquil you are relaxed.

But relaxation is not necessarily tranquillity. We can be relaxed while the mind is going through a peaceful daydream, or while it is recalling the pleasant memories of last summer, or while it is drifting in and out of a light sleep. All these states are joyful experiences, and of great value in themselves. But they are not states of tranquillity. Our peaceful thoughts are still thoughts, and we are still pursuing them instead of holding the mind in the stillness of its own being.

ACHIEVING TRANQUILLITY

Does the simple act of watching the breath automatically put us into this state of tranquillity? Certainly, if we are able to just watch the breath. But for most of us the one-pointedness of watching the breath is a new experience for the mind. The mind isn't used to it. It is used to chasing its own thoughts, and dominating our lives from morning till night. So once you start sitting in meditation and watching your breath, your mind will do all it can to distract you.

It will see this one-pointedness, this bare attention as a threat to its power. It will tug at your sleeve

LEFT IF YOU ARE A PAINTER, YOUR MIND MAY TRY TO DISTRACT YOU BY SUGGESTING PICTURES TO YOU. DON'T WORRY THAT YOU WILL LOSE THESE CREATIVE INSIGHTS IF YOU CONTINUE WITH YOUR MEDITATION.

with first one thought and then another. It will try to tempt you with happy thoughts, unsettle you with sad ones, distract you with anxious ones, remind you of all the things you have to do or should be doing, and – if all else fails – it will throw in a few erotic thoughts.

And it will call up emotions to help. It will bring back the emotion you felt earlier in the day when someone was unpleasant to you, or the emotion you felt when someone was kind. It will remind you of the warm feelings you had when you did a good turn for someone. It will conjure up pictures, visions, scenes sometimes from actual experience and sometimes from fantasy. It will show you snow-capped mountains, dark forests, winding pathways, the strangely carved roofs of houses, castles glimpsed through the mist, the sea open and shining under a sunlit sky. It will make these visions so entrancing that you may well mistake them for the scenery of your journey, and imagine that these are places you have come to see.

ABOVE IF YOUR TALENTS ARE OF A MUSICAL NATURE, YOUR MIND MAY TRY TO DISTRACT YOU WITH THE PROMISE OF NEW TUNES.

66

And if none of these things enable it to recapture your attention, it will give you creative insights, solutions to problems that have long been puzzling you. If you are a writer it will give you ideas for your book or your poem, if you are a musician it will hum new tunes. It will urge you to get up and put these things on paper before they fade. It will mislead you into thinking that at the end of meditation, they will have vanished without trace.

The mind is indeed often at its most creative in meditation, but for the present you are meditating, and each of these distractions must simply be observed as it arises and then passes away. Be assured, however, that if you mentally tab any insights worth remembering, they will come back to you once the meditation is over.

THE VALUE OF THINKING

Simply because they interfere with meditation, don't imagine that all of these distractions are necessarily bad. Thoughts, emotions, feelings, memories, ideas are all vital to us, in spite of the fact that in meditation we refer to them as distractions.

Even the chatter inside our heads is an essential part of life. We need to weigh up problems, to work out what we are going to do and say, to go over past experiences and see what we can learn from them, to amuse ourselves with memories, to imagine the future. We would be less than human if we didn't satisfy this need. And we would be failing to make proper use of that excellent tool, the thinking mind.

Thought is one of the great gifts of the human race and, for the most part, it is still only little understood and used. And for this very reason, meditation is an aid to thought. Meditation is the friend of thought. Meditation shows us that it is not thought that is wrong, but our uncontrolled way of thinking. We have allowed thought to become chaotic, to dominate rather than to serve. Meditation helps us to make better use of our thinking, to allow it to become part of the clearness rather than the confusion.

The tranquillity experienced in meditation – and you will observe this happening relatively early in your practice – will begin to spread into your daily life. And as it does so you will find that the mind becomes less cluttered, that you are able to think more quickly and more clearly, that you will be able to look at issues more objectively, examine arguments more thoroughly, see through problems more readily.

Meditation will not make you a genius, but it will help you use thoughts more effectively.

Now let's look at the third stage in the meditation journey: insight.

INSIGHT

As I said earlier, tranquillity and insight are part of each other. They're rather like your two feet. When you walk, your weight is first on one foot and then on the other, but walking depends on both feet working together as one, as a unity. Without this unity, walking would be impossible. Neither foot is more important than the other, neither foot can function separately from the other.

But what is insight?

Insight means seeing in a special way into the true nature of something.

But the true nature of what?

The answer is, we see into the nature of ourselves. We see who we are. Not (unless we are very lucky) in one blinding flash, but little by little, like seeing first one part of a picture, then another, then another, and adding further pieces until in the end we have the whole picture.

Many meditators warn that in meditation you come not upon a knowing but upon a 'not knowing', an insight into the mystery of existence which is experienced rather than known. They will also warn that the very idea of knowledge gets in

ABOVE AS YOUR FEET MUST WORK TOGETHER IN ORDER FOR YOU TO WALK, SO TRANQUILLITY AND INSIGHT MUST WORK TOGETHER, AS A UNITY.

LEFT HAVING DEVELOPED YOUR SKILLS OF CONCENTRATION AND ACHIEVED A STATE OF TRANQUILLITY, YOU MAY FIND THAT INSIGHT FOLLOWS.

the way, because it suggests that there is something that can be understood and written down and told to others.

Many Zen masters, for example, insist on keeping what they call a 'don't know' mind, a mind which is open instead of a mind which wants to categorize and label things, like specimens in a museum. They will tell you that you are free to categorize and label if you wish, but you will end up knowing only your categories and labels, and not the things that are categorized and labelled. Once we think we 'know', we close our minds to anything else, instead of waiting to see what experience brings. These warnings are important. So, when developing insight, look for a sense of awareness rather than for a knowledge of 'facts' which can be reduced to simple statements.

Look for an awareness which has more of an 'ah yes I see' about it than an 'ah yes I know'.

But where does this awareness start? Having begun to work with concentration, and having developed something of tranquillity, how do we develop our insight? Is there a recognized place where we should begin? You can in fact begin at any one of a number of different points, but as you are already working with your breathing, let's stay with this.

INSIGHT INTO BREATHING

Breathing is so automatic for us that we are very rarely aware of what breath is, or of how we are breathing. We are ignorant in so many ways of the very process upon which life depends. If someone or something were to stop us from breathing, in a moment we would become aware that the ability to take our next breath is the most important and sweetest experience in the world. If someone or something were to stop us from breathing, in a moment we would be fighting desperately for our very existence. Ask a person who has nearly drowned how important breathing is.

So in meditation, since you are concentrating on your breathing, examine it closely and try to answer these questions:

Are you breaths long or short?
Do they feel rough or smooth, harsh or soft, tense or relaxed?

Become one with your breathing. Feel it from the inside, identify with it so that you and your breathing are not separate.

During this exercise, don't struggle to change the pattern of your breathing. But once you have gained some insight into it, allow it to lose any tension you may have found. We are so unaware of our breathing that we aren't conscious of the way we alter its natural inflow and out-flow. We may do this by narrowing the air passages

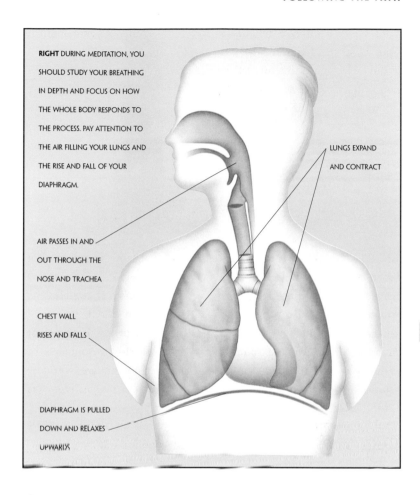

RIGHT DURING MEDITATION, YOU SHOULD STUDY YOUR BREATHING IN DEPTH AND FOCUS ON HOW THE WHOLE BODY RESPONDS TO THE PROCESS. PAY ATTENTION TO THE AIR FILLING YOUR LUNGS AND THE RISE AND FALL OF YOUR DIAPHRAGM.

LUNGS EXPAND AND CONTRACT

AIR PASSES IN AND OUT THROUGH THE NOSE AND TRACHEA

CHEST WALL RISES AND FALLS

DIAPHRAGM IS PULLED DOWN AND RELAXES UPWARDS

through which it passes, or by interrupting its rhythm. In meditation you can become aware that this is happening. While remaining focused on the nostrils or the abdomen, allow your awareness gently to widen, until it registers how the rest of your body is responding to your breathing. Don't confuse this exercise with actually allowing your awareness to follow your breathing, like a pet dog following its master or mistress. Think more in terms of a bird soaring into the sky and, though still gazing at the same spot on the ground, taking in more and more of the countryside as its field of vision widens.

VIPASSANA

Different systems of meditation may have different names, but basically they all centre around concentration, tranquillity and insight. The practice I have described so far, in which the meditator's attention is drawn to these three stages, is usually called 'vipassana'. Let's remind ourselves what vipassana is.

CONCENTRATION

In concentration, the meditator draws all the scattered parts of their attention together and focuses, clearly and calmly, upon a single thing – at first the breathing. Whenever the mind wanders, it is brought gently back to this point of focus. By degrees, as the mind becomes concentrated in this way, it calms down, and becomes tranquil.

TRANQUILLITY

This tranquillity is not a sleepy or trance-like state, but instead an alert condition during which one's usual worries and anxieties no longer have control. This leads to a state of clarity in which insight occurs.

INSIGHT

Insight occurs at many different levels, but at first involves a growing awareness of one's own existence, and of the temporary nature of emotions and thoughts. Eventually, it can result in an awareness of the still centre of one's own being, of who and what one is.

Vipassana meditation can be practised anywhere. You only have to bring your attention clearly and firmly to your breathing, and hold it there, to experience the beginnings of tranquillity and insight. It is important that you should be able to do this wherever you happen to be, but regular practice, at a definite time and place each day, is vital if you are to go further with your meditation.

THE MEANING OF THE PALI TERMS

Vipassana means 'insight'

Sattipatana means 'concentration'

Samatha means 'tranquillity'

In the West, only the term vipassana is in frequent use.

Work with this insight into your breathing until it becomes a natural and regular part of your meditation. At some point during this growing insight, you will find you are able to stop counting your breaths. But even though you can now leave counting behind, be ready to return to it on those occasions when your mind for any reason is so busy that you again need the help it can give. When this happens, don't think you are slipping back. Counting is something you carry with you on your journey, to make use of whenever the need arises.

As your practice becomes more established you will notice that your breathing automatically becomes softer, gentler, more subtle, until at times you hardly notice it. Don't be tempted to interfere with this or to tell yourself that you should be taking longer breaths. This new way of breathing is a sign that your body is responding well to your meditation. As the body becomes more efficient you require less oxygen. Your body has its own wisdom, and adjusts these things for itself. You will find it helpful, however, to take several deep slow breaths as a preparation for meditation once you're settled on your cushion. Release any tensions you may be feeling along with the out-breaths. Don't take too many of these deep breaths though. Three or four are enough. Putting too much oxygen into the bloodstream can

ABOVE AWARENESS SHOULD EXPAND SLOWLY OVER BODY – HERE STARTING AT THE NOSTRILS AND MOVING ON TO THE FACE, THE NECK AND THE ABDOMEN.

lead to feelings of light-headedness, one of the last things you want while in meditation.

Some meditation schools also teach the value of swaying the body slowly from left to right until you settle in an upright pose Experiment with this. If it helps you, use it. Sway three or four times to left and right, reducing the distance you sway each time, until you finish in your upright meditation position. This can help the body to feel more settled and more ready to begin the process of insight. Don't see it as a piece of baggage that you leave behind as your journey progresses.

ABOVE HERE THE AWARENESS OR ATTENTION IS SWEEPING OVER THE BODY, STARTING AT THE TOP OF THE HEAD AND MOVING DOWN OVER THE FACE, NECK, SHOULDERS, ARMS AND SO ON.

OTHER FORMS OF INSIGHT

Once you are able to keep focused on your breathing and develop insight into it for fifteen minutes at a time, you are ready to focus your insight on to other areas as well.

Stay with the body at first. Remember that your body is an important part of your reality, it is where your mind and spirit live. Chapter 1 listed some of the benefits that come to the body through meditation. Don't underestimate their importance. And there are other benefits, less obvious but of equal value, which have to do with a sense of being more at home in your body, of seeing mind, body and spirit as one. These benefits lead you to be more welcoming towards your body, to respect it and its genuine needs, to experience it in new, more balanced and more harmonious ways.

AWARENESS EXPANDS OVER THE BODY

The first exercise, as with the insight into breathing, is to allow your awareness to expand from its point of focus at the nostrils or the abdomen until it covers the whole body. You may not be able to do this all at once. At first, you may find your attention skips back and forth between your point of focus and the other parts of your body. Simply note this, in the same objective way you note everything else in meditation. Then take your attention back to your breathing and try again.

Don't try to go too fast. Allow your awareness to broaden until (if your original point of focus is the nostrils) you are aware of your face. Later, try to take this awareness further down, to the neck, then to the chest, then to the abdomen. Try to feel the body both from the inside (the sense of being in the body) and from the outside (the sense of being in contact with whatever is outside the body).

As your awareness broadens, so the details that you are aware of may become less sharp. Nevertheless you should find a kind of very subtle overall awareness developing, so that without quite knowing how it happens you have a feeling of wholeness, of a unified body instead of a collection of physical parts somehow held together.

This sense of being more at home in your body comes about naturally once you have set up a pattern of meditation, but it's greatly helped if you develop insight into your physical self. This is done by 'feeling' your body both from the

LEFT CONCENTRATE ON THE SENSATIONS IN BOTH OF YOUR HANDS. TRY TO ESTABLISH WHETHER YOU CAN FEEL EACH HAND INDEPENDENTLY OF THE OTHER.

inside and at those points where it touches the outside world. There are two exercises for doing this, both of which you should practise.

AWARENESS SWEEPS OVER THE BODY

The second exercise for gaining insight into the body, which you may find easier, is to allow the awareness to sweep the body, slowly and in minute details, again trying to feel from both the inside and from the outside.

In this technique, you deliberately allow your attention to move from its point of focus at the nostrils or the abdomen and to travel around the surface of the body.

Start by directing your awareness to the top of your head. The scalp is well supplied with blood and nerve endings, and is a very sensitive area. Become aware of a point on your head. Can you feel something there? A slight tingling? Maybe the sensation of blood flowing?

If you can't feel anything, don't worry. Your nerves are quite capable of registering these sensations. Notice, for example, how quickly they notice anything unusual, even the lightest tickling by a feather. But they have become used to the normal sensations of the body, and no longer register them. This is right and proper. You wouldn't want to feel these sensations all the time. But increased awareness of your own body means that you become able to feel them when you want to feel them.

Now, whether you can feel these sensations on your head or not, allow the awareness, with focused concentration, to travel around the rest of the body. Allow it to move down to the face. What can you feel there?

Usually it's quite easy to become aware of the sensation of the closed eyelids, of the lips pressing gently against each other, of the tongue behind the teeth. Now move down to the jaw and the neck, now the shoulders. What are the sensations there? Again can you feel the flow of blood, the sensation of the skin against the air or against your clothes? (Don't move any part of the body to exaggerate these sensations; try to feel them just as they are.)

Now move down the arms, now into the hands. Feel the hands resting against each other or on your knees. If they are resting against each other, which hand are you aware of? Can you be aware of them both at once? If so, can you feel them together as a single sensation?

Now sweep the rest of the body: the back, the abdomen, the buttocks resting on your cushion, the genitals, the thighs, the legs and feet. Feel each part of the body in turn with your awareness, almost as if you were stroking it sensitively with the tips of your fingers.

If you have any aches, pains or feelings of discomfort, investigate them with the same light touch. Don't label them as 'bad' or 'good', no matter how strong the urge to do so. Investigate them for what they are. What is this feeling? Don't attempt to answer with words. Just be aware of the sensation, and allow your answer to be direct experience, nothing more, nothing less. This practice is important in providing you with insight into the nature of sensation and in controlling pain.

78

Part of the reason we experience pain as so unpleasant is that we fight against it, we tense our muscles around it, we resist it with all our might, we give it names so that it has even more power over us. Once you are able just to investigate pain, to relax into it, you may become aware that the pain is 'only that'. This doesn't mean that pain isn't real, just that you can start to take control over it and stop it filling your mind.

IMPORTANCE OF INSIGHT PRACTICE

You don't have to carry out the above two insight exercises each time you meditate. You don't even need to carry them out for the whole of a meditation session. You may decide to spend the first part of the session watching the breath and working with concentration and tranquillity, then move to the experience of insight, then back into concentration and tranquillity. (Eventually, all three things will tend to be happening at the same time anyway.) But do make sure that you include regular insight practice. Tranquillity can become so pleasant that it seems an effort to carry out insight practice.

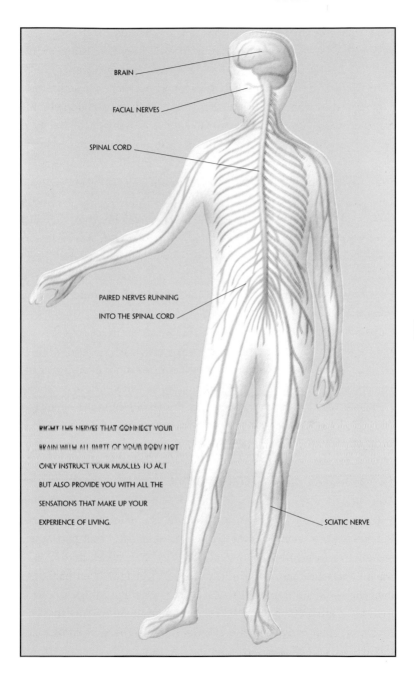

BRAIN

FACIAL NERVES

SPINAL CORD

PAIRED NERVES RUNNING
INTO THE SPINAL CORD

SCIATIC NERVE

RIGHT THE NERVES THAT CONNECT YOUR
BRAIN WITH ALL PARTS OF YOUR BODY NOT
ONLY INSTRUCT YOUR MUSCLES TO ACT
BUT ALSO PROVIDE YOU WITH ALL THE
SENSATIONS THAT MAKE UP YOUR
EXPERIENCE OF LIVING.

If you only ever remain in tranquillity, you will only ever experience some of the benefits of meditation. And if you are not very careful, your tranquillity will be less clear and become just a cosy, enjoyable state to go into – and this is the very opposite of·what you really want.

INSIGHT INTO EMOTIONS

Having tasted a little of what insight means for the body, it is now time to look at your emotions. The emotions, although they come from the mind, are felt by the body. Meditation helps you deal with emotions not by fighting them but by giving you insight into their real nature. Meditation helps you to see that emotions are physical sensations, and as physical sensations they can be controlled by the mind.

ABOVE THE FEELINGS EXPERIENCED BY A SPORTSPERSON IN THE MIDST OF COMPETITION ARE ACTUALLY VERY SIMILAR TO THOSE FELT BY SOMEONE WHO IS SCARED.

INVESTIGATING EMOTIONS

Gaining insight into your emotions means investigating them much in the way that you investigated other bodily sensations. It means looking closely at them, and as one looks, seeing that these emotions, these dreaded things like fear, anxiety, guilt, anger, have no real substance at all. They are just temporary physical feelings which we have chosen to label in certain ways.

As we look at these feelings, so we can see that some of the ones our mind label as opposites are in fact remarkably similar. Fear and excitement, for example, produce identical butterflies in the stomach, identical dryness in the mouth, identical sweating in the palms.

Once you begin to look into the real nature of your emotions you will find that they 'open out'. They dissolve – sometimes into laughter – and lose something of the power which they once had over you.

PREPARING FOR EMOTIONS

You will also find that your increased sensitivity means that in everyday life you now become aware of these emotions as they begin to arise, instead of only when they have taken control. This allows you to relax physically and so avoid the full force of the emotion. You can learn to switch off – the emotion starts to arise, you see it for what it is and allow it to fall away.

CAUSES OF EMOTIONS

More importantly still, this increased sensitivity will help you to see what it is in the mind that sets off the emotions. You may begin to see that your anger is born of defensiveness, from the fear that someone is attacking your professional pride or your possessions or your sense of personal worth. Or you may see that your fear is triggered by the thought that something awful is going to happen, or your guilt by the thought you 'deserve' to be punished.

These thoughts may happen so quickly, and you may be so used to thinking them, that normally you don't know they are there. It's only as your insight grows as a result of meditation that you're able to see them. You can then decide whether there is good reason for the emotions or whether they are ridiculous, and can therefore be put away.

WORKING WITH EMOTIONS

You can also work with emotions if and when they happen to arise during meditation itself, or you can decide deliberately to bring the emotions to your mind, for example by remembering something upsetting that happened recently. If you use the latter method, decide before the meditation starts that this is what you are going to do. (Once you have started to meditate, your mind should not be making such decisions.) Tell yourself as you get into your meditation position that as soon as you have focused the mind you will look at the upsetting event that brought about the emotion.

Once the mind is focused and the event arises from the memory, you will often find that it no longer upsets you. This is fine. It shows how tranquil you are. And it will help you to avoid upset when similar things happen.

On the other hand, you may find that as the memory comes to you, you feel upset again. This is fine too. It will help you to look at the upset and see what caused it. Does it come from your feeling of being unfairly treated? Of being victimized? Of being neglected or slighted or ridiculed? Look at where it comes from – don't judge this or start to think about what you should do next time you feel this way. Don't try to deny what you may now recognize as your own emotional over-reactions. Simply note where the feeling comes from. You can return to the subject after the meditation is over. If you find you get nowhere with this information after your meditation, decide to look at the emotion again next time you meditate. Eventually things will become clearer.

Insight into Thoughts

Moving from insight into the body to insight into the emotions to insight into thoughts is to follow an increasingly subtle path on your journey. You may have found it quite easy to gain insight into the body, and slightly more difficult to do the same with your emotions. You may find it more difficult still with thoughts. Perhaps 'difficult' is the wrong word, since it suggests the need for more effort. In fact, you will need more patience. The actual process of gaining insight is the same for the body, the emotions and the thoughts.

LOOKING AT THOUGHTS

When working with insight into thoughts, you should start with concentration and tranquillity as usual. You should start to look at your thoughts. Watch them arise and pass with the same calm, objective attention that you use when watching your breath. Don't become attached to any thought. Don't try and hold on to it. If a particular thought refuses to go, you can, in your imagination, give it a nudge. If it still refuses to move on, stare at it in the way you stared at your emotions. See that it is just a set of words or pictures that your mind has created out of nothing.

LABELLING THOUGHTS

Although we usually avoid labelling in meditation, you can, if necessary, label your thoughts. Use your own choice of labels, but they should involve emotional terms like 'frightening', 'exciting', 'intimidating', 'challenging' and so on, and also terms like 'memory', 'planning ahead', 'regretting' and 'hoping'.

Labelling helps with insight here, because it allows you to see the patterns that your thoughts follow. Are you thinking positively about yourself, about your life, about your relationships, or thinking negatively? Do you notice a pattern of resentful thoughts towards others, or of jealous thoughts, or of envious ones? Look at what is happening.

PATTERNS OF THINKING

Your pattern of thinking tells you a great deal about yourself. As you begin to see this pattern, don't react to it, or judge it. See it for what it is, an insight into your own nature. Don't try to plan during your meditation what you are going to do with this insight. Note it, and leave it until after the meditation before you start to explore what it is telling you, and what this means for your future action.

Don't be disappointed if you appear to make no progress with this, and if your thoughts still seem to be mysterious to you. Answers in meditation often arise when we least expect them.

CAUSES OF THOUGHTS

If you want to go deeper, you need to know what is bringing these thoughts about. We spend so much of our lives thinking but where do our thoughts actually come from? What lies beneath them? What is it in us that sets them off? What is it in you, for example, that brings about feelings of regret, that makes you cling to memories, that urges you to plan ahead, that gives you hope? What parts of yourself are you looking at when you see the thoughts that give rise to these feelings coming into being?

The answers are particular to each one of us, and only make real sense when we discover them for ourselves. But these answers must not be sought in the way you seek answers to the usual questions of life. You should not make an effort to find an answer, don't look through a set of different possibilities. The answers should be felt rather than expressed. The answers may come through symbols, pictures, impressions, through an inner awareness that emerges without going through a step-by-step search for the answer. It will be more of a revelation if you like. Once you think you have an answer, see whether it still works in real life and in your next session of meditation. Don't see the answer as 'permanent'. There will be other, deeper revelations to come.

UNFORMED THOUGHTS

As you advance in meditation, you will find that thoughts begin to lose their ability to enter into your awareness. You may experience periods without thinking, and during this time you may feel what can be described as the 'energy' of unformed thoughts pressing against your awareness, but as if the energy involved is no longer strong enough to break through. When this happens, investigate this energy with a relaxed, watchful curiosity. What is it, what does it represent, where is it coming from?

Don't be disappointed if you appear to make no progress with this, and if your thoughts still seem to by mysterious to you. Answers in meditation often arise when we least expect them.

OTHER WAYS OF TRAVELLING

CHAPTER SIX

So far I have discussed travelling with a focus on your breath, your bodily sensations, your emotions and your thoughts. It is now time to look at other ways of travelling.

Remember not to rush to try a range of different meditation techniques to see if they 'work'. Try each one carefully first. If you try everything at once, you will only be confused and you will lose the energy and motivation you need to keep going.

Read through the techniques on the following pages, but only use them when the time is right. With each technique, I will try to show the relationship with the three key stages of concentration, tranquillity and insight. When you do decide to work with them they will therefore fit in with what you have already learnt, rather than being something completely new.

TRAVELLING WITH COLOUR

If you are good at visualizing colours, you may choose to use this exercise as an alternative to counting, in order to keep the attention focused on the breath.

Use counting first and then replace the seven numbers with the colours of the rainbow. Visualize red as you enter meditation and breathe out your first breath, orange as you breathe out your second, yellow as you breathe out your third, and so on up to violet. For breaths eight, nine and ten visualize two colours each time, a primary colour with what artists call its complementary colour (i.e. the colour formed from the combination of the two other primary colours) in each case. So visualize red with green, yellow with violet and blue with orange. These combinations are harder to visualize than combinations of a primary colour and one of its derivatives (e.g. blue with green), and are therefore more useful in keeping the mind in a state of alertness.

When carrying out this exercise, try not to think of the name of the colour or colours as you visualize them.

After working with these colours, you may choose to work with just one colour for a whole meditation session. You can then see the effect that each colour has upon your concentration, tranquillity, and if – and how – it influences your feelings both during and after the session.

Colour can affect both our moods and our thoughts, and gaining insight into what colours mean for each of us individually is an important part of extending our self-understanding.

To work this way, concentrate on the breathing as usual, but have your chosen colour as a background to the breathing. Imagine yourself surrounded softly by the colour, as if your breath is coming to you through a tunnel formed by and through it. If at any time this practice becomes disturbing, discontinue the visualization and return simply to your breathing, saying to yourself:

*'The white light
of my breathing
banishes all colours,
and surrounds me
in peace'.*

TRAVELLING WITH SOUND

Sound can have profound effects upon our minds. We notice this especially with music. Some music soothes, some music energizes, and some music simply annoys.

We also notice it in the sounds of everyday life. We enjoy the sound of water, of waves and waterfalls, of the wind in the trees, of birdsong, of the low rumble of distant thunder. We enjoy the sound of human voices, of a baby chuckling, of laughter. Other sounds, though they are nothing special in themselves, we enjoy through association – the chink of teacups, the cork popping from the wine bottle, the gentle ripple of applause, the lawnmower in the distance – the gentle sounds of summer.

By contrast, we tend to dislike harsh, sudden, invasive or discordant sounds. Such sounds are useful in that they teach us the value of silence, but whereas pleasant sounds can soothe or excite, unpleasant sounds grate upon the nerves and can produce anger, fear and frustration, and can even leave us feeling disturbed and disorientated.

It is not surprising therefore, that sound can be used to great effect in meditation. Chanting, songs and sacred music are all designed to put us into an altered state of consciousness. When we put sound and meditation together, the result can be very deep and far-reaching.

RIGHT THE SOUND OF A HAPPY BABY WILL PUT US INTO A CERTAIN MOOD. CONTRAST THIS WITH THE EFFECT OF A CRYING BABY AND THE INFLUENCE OF SOUND BECOMES CLEAR.

MANTRAS

One way of using sound is to employ a mantra. These were originally used in the Hindu tradition and consisted of lines from the ancient Vedic sutras or hymns. They allowed the mind to consider sacred truths until these truths 'revealed' themselves to the meditator and took on a deep inner meaning. However in more recent centuries, and particularly in Buddhist traditions, mantras have been used as much for the quality of the sounds they contain as for any meaning carried by the individual words.

In fact, since many of the most widely used mantras are in Sanskrit or Tibetan, they are not understood by the majority of those who use them, particularly Westerners. Some of the sounds used in a mantra – such as 'om', 'hum' and 'swaha' – do not in fact have any direct meaning. They are sound for the sake of sound.

When working with a mantra, the syllables are repeated rhythmically, either aloud or to oneself, over and over again. Sometimes this is done with the help of a mala, a string of 108 beads which is held in the right hand and worked slowly through the fingers, with each bead held briefly on each repetition. Whether or not a mala is used, the mantra is best combined with the breathing, with a repetition occurring on each in-breath and each out-breath.

Instead of consisting of phrases, some mantras involve just a single word, which can be repeated a number of times on each in-breath and each out-breath, or which can be used independently of the

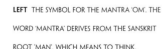

LEFT THE SYMBOL FOR THE MANTRA 'OM'. THE WORD 'MANTRA' DERIVES FROM THE SANSKRIT ROOT 'MAN', WHICH MEANS TO THINK.

breathing. If you are saying the mantra silently to yourself rather than out loud, it is nevertheless useful to say it out loud a few times at the beginning of each meditation, gradually reducing the sound to a whisper. This helps to establish the sound in one's mind, and the practice can be repeated during the meditation itself if the attention is found to wander.

DOES MISPRONUNCIATION MATTER?

An ancient Sufi story tells of a sternly orthodox Dervish teacher, who walking one day beside the riverbank, heard someone from a hermitage on one of the islands chanting a Dervish mantra. 'That is no good', thought the Dervish to himself, 'the fellow is mispronouncing it.' Whereupon he hired a boat, rowed out to the island, and informed the hermit that instead of chanting 'U ya hu' he should be chanting 'Ya hu'.

The hermit humbly thanked the Dervish, who then returned to his boat and set off back, feeling very pleased with himself for his kind deed. After all, it was taught that if the mantras were chanted correctly one could even walk on water, though he had never himself been fortunate enough to witness the feat.

The silence from the island assured the Dervish that the hermit was now digesting the lesson he had just been given. But a few moments later a faltering 'U ya hu' floating over the water revealed that the hermit was, in spite of himself, unable to shake off his old bad habits. The Dervish rested on his oars, and was reflecting on the frailty of his fellow men when a strange sight met his eyes. The hermit had now left his island and was walking over the water towards the rowing boat. 'I'm sorry to trouble you brother' he said hesitantly, 'but I have come to ask you once again to tell me the correct method of pronunciation, for I have difficulty in remembering it.'

DOES THE CHOICE OF SOUND MATTER?

As a young boy walking to school one day I noticed the road sign to London, and for some reason began repeating 'London' to myself over and over again. I still remember the surprise I felt when I realized that such a familiar name lost its associations in the process, and became simply a sound, a sound which seemed, as I continued with the repetitions, to strip associations briefly away from language itself, leaving me with a strange yet pleasant feeling of being one with everything around me. As the objects surrounding me lost their linguistic labels, so they lost the concepts that went with these labels, and became without boundaries, merging and flowing into each other and I with and into them.

The teaching in most traditions is that you should be given your mantra by your meditation teacher. In the Tibetan Buddhist system the mantra is usually associated with a particular buddha or bodhisattva, in some Hindu systems the teacher chooses a mantra which is claimed to be particularly appropriate to you personally, or in Christian traditions you are taught the value of a particular short prayer, and instructed to repeat it a set number of times each day.

Some people worry about the pronunciation of their mantra, but I believe that your dedication to practice is more important. In fact any succession of rhythmical sounds, no matter how meaningless, will put the mind in the right state if repeated often enough and with the necessary focused awareness. This can be equally true of sounds which do have meaning, since the repetition can often strip this meaning away, and leave one working with the pure sound alone.

If you do not have a meditation teacher to choose a mantra for you, you can take any sound that you find has a particular appeal. It can be a word such as 'peace', or a phrase such as 'peace is in and with me'. Or you can take the name of one of the great spiritual teachers.

Another alternative is to use the sound 'om' (written more phonetically as 'aum') on its own. This sound has been claimed for thousands of years to be the 'universal' sound, the essence of all sounds, and as such to have a profound effect upon the mind. When using it on its own, you can obtain the full quality of the range of sounds it contains by beginning with a long 'a' (pronounced like the 'a' in 'father') in the back of the throat, continuing with the 'u' (pronounced 'oo') in the middle of the mouth, and terminating with a 'm' sound at the front of the mouth behind closed lips. Each sound should resonate or vibrate.

These resonations and vibrations can be felt through the whole body by making the initial 'a' resonate in the belly, the middle 'oo' resonate and vibrate in the chest, and the final 'm' vibrate in the skull, at the point above and behind the eyes. The whole sound should occupy the complete out-breath, and after several audible repetitions of it you will find that your body feels invigorated and energized, yet at the same time relaxed and centred.

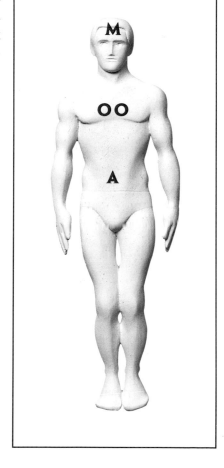

RIGHT ANYONE WHO DOUBTS THE VALUE OF SOUND SHOULD TRY USING THESE SOUNDS AND FEEL THE RESULTS FOR THEMSELVES.

DANGERS OF MEDITATION

Are there any dangers in meditation?

If repeating your name over and over as a mantra can result in the word losing its meaning, can this result in depersonalization?

Can meditation lead us to lose touch with reality?

Can we come across levels of our own mind such as repressed memories or emotions that we find disturbing?

It would be wrong to suggest that dangers don't exist. Almost everything in life carries certain dangers. Books and films can upset and disturb us. Relationships can upset and disturb us. Even wholesome food can upset and disturb us. But the dangers of meditation are not great provided one travels at the right speed, and provided one always remembers that meditation is a way of gaining insight into reality rather than a way of escaping from reality. Let's look at one or two of these dangers in more detail.

DEPERSONALIZATION

There's no doubt that, if we go into a trance-like state in meditation instead of keeping the mind alert and focused, we can feel disorientated when we emerge from it. We may not know where we are and may feel that we have lost touch with the world and with our own identity. This is not unlike the depersonalization we may experience if woken suddenly from a deep sleep.

The lesson to be learnt is simple. Keep the mind always aware of what it is you're doing. If you're watching the breath, then watch the breath. If visualizing a colour, visualize a colour, and so on.

Chanting, mantra meditation, and exercises such as repeating your own name over and over again are more likely to lead to depersonalization than watching the breath. If you find this is the case, stay with the breath. Your breath will always ground you, will always calm and reassure you.

EXTRA-SENSORY PERCEPTION

Most of the great meditation traditions teach that meditators sometimes find themselves gaining powers of extra-sensory perception such as telepathy and clairvoyance at a certain stage in their practice. These powers can become a distraction, and should therefore simply be observed (or used occasionally when they are helpful to others), rather than being employed for our own good or seen as a source of pride.

Science has always been divided on the existence of extra-sensory perception. Some scientists regard it as proven virtually beyond doubt by carefully controlled experiments, others dismiss it as superstition. The only way to resolve the issue for oneself is through personal experience.

When you start to meditate, you may find your dreams become more vivid, that you recall them more clearly upon waking, and that you even have lucid dreams (those dreams in which we are consciously aware that we are dreaming) and out-of-the-body experiences. Sometimes information may come to you in these dreams which you feel is telepathic or clairvoyant. In waking life, you may have sudden flashes of intuition.

Note these things, and see what they appear to mean and to prove. But remember, they are just a part of, not the purpose of, your meditation practice.

93

TRAVELLING WITH PICTURES

Another stimulus that can be used during meditation is pictures or geometrical patterns or shapes, either observed directly or held in the mind as visualizations. Let's take those observed directly first.

Since you don't want to give the mind too much temptation to stray it's better not to use pictures of something in particular for this purpose. Instead, use geometrical shapes and patterns.

ABOVE GEOMETRICAL SHAPES OR PATTERNS CAN BE USED AS A STIMULUS DURING MEDITATION.

THE CIRCLE

The circle is the simplest of geometric shapes and yet has been used for centuries to symbolize wholeness, totality, completion, perfection, fulfilment, the rhythm of life, the constant outgoing and returning of existence, the unity of all things, the absolute. If a dot is placed at its centre, this represents the still point in the middle, and the circle now symbolizes motion, change, yet at the same time the absence of change. The circle can spin on its axis, yet, however fast it moves it still remains a circle, and each point on its circumference remains an equally valuable part of the whole.

The circle also symbolizes form and emptiness, emptiness and form. The circumference of the circle encloses empty space, yet the space inside and outside the circumference can be said to enclose the circumference. What, therefore, defines the circle? The circumference or the space, the form or the emptiness?

Because of these rich symbolic meanings, the circle provides an ideal focus for meditation. But be clear how symbols like the circle

95

work. They do not work through the meaning you attach to them. When meditating on a circle don't concentrate on the interpretations of the symbol such as I've just referred to. The symbol of the circle speaks directly to you, and only afterwards do you find the need to translate its language into words. Symbols such as the circle hold a power in and of themselves. Certain symbols appear to be keys which put us into closer touch with our own unconscious. They occur to us in dreams, and by holding them in our minds we are able to experience their power to heal, to inform, to calm the mind, to broaden its boundaries and to take us into deeper and deeper levels of our own consciousnes.

RIGHT ALTHOUGH THE CIRCLE HAS A HUGE NUMBER OF ASSOCIATIONS, IT IS NOT THESE THAT YOU SHOULD CONCENTRATE ON WHEN USING THE CIRCLE FOR MEDITATION.

When meditating on the circle, draw it boldly in black on a white background, and place a small dot in the centre. You can use colour if you prefer, but remember that colour carries its own meaning. At the moment, you want simply to respond to the circle as a shape. Make the circle relatively large (at least 30 centimetres – 1 foot – in diameter), and place it on the wall at eye-level to yourself as you are sitting ready to meditate. Begin your meditation by focusing for a moment on your breathing, then gaze steadily at the circle. Blink when you eyes become uncomfortable, but otherwise keep blinking to a minimum.

At first, notice how your mind wants to pull away from the circle and go in search of something more 'exciting'. Notice it, but allow it to make no difference to your steady gazing. Notice too how all kinds of everyday associations to do with the circle will leap into your mind. Allow them to come and go, as you do with any other thoughts. Observe them but pay no particular attention to them.

They are simply the attempt by your mind to make 'sense' of what you're seeing. You are not interested in this attempt, because you are focusing on the circle itself, not on ideas about circles. As your meditation deepens, more profound insights will start to emerge. Don't become excited by them. Simply observe them, as you do with more trivial thoughts. They will come back to your mind again after the meditation if they are worth remembering. Don't allow yourself to feel you are meditating in order to discover some profound secret. You are meditating on the circle because it is a circle and because you are meditating, nothing more, nothing less.

After some practice in this meditation you will notice that the circle is having its own effect upon your life. It may be helping you towards greater tranquillity in your daily affairs. It may be influencing your dream life. It may be giving you insights into your self that you had not thought possible.

These things are for you to discover. It is of no value to dictate expectations to you. These will simply get in the way of your journey.

THE CROSS

Another geometric shape to have figured in symbolism through the centuries is the cross. It traditionally symbolizes the point of communication between heaven and earth; but also symbolizes the universal man, the tree of life, male and female, the union of opposites, the descent of spirit into matter, the four rivers of paradise, the four elements united at a fifth central point.

ABOVE THE CROSS IS A SYMBOLIC SHAPE FOR MANY RELIGIONS.

THE TRIANGLE

The traditional symbolism associated with the triangle is usually concerned with the threefold nature of the universe (heaven, earth, and humankind). Three triangles combined together form a star, the symbolism of highest attainment, the messenger of God, the presence of divinity.

97

These three shapes, the circle, the cross and the triangle, have been combined in a number of ways by the various traditions. For example the circle enclosing the cross has often been taken to represent the union of heaven and earth, the circle at the centre of the cross solar power and majesty, and the triangle in the circle the plane of forms held within the circle of eternity. The square is also sometimes added to these combinations.

You can work on these shapes yourself combining them in various different ways until you find something that seems to have direct meaning for you personally. How will you know when this meaning arises? Look for a particular sense of

RIGHT YOU MAY FIND THAT PARTICULAR COMBINATIONS OF GEOMETRIC SHAPES TAKE ON A SPECIAL MEANING FOR YOU.

ABOVE AS WITH ALL PICTURES AND SHAPES, IT IS IMPORTANT THAT YOU DO NOT DWELL ON THE MEANING OF
THE SRICAKRA, RATHER ALLOW THE FORM TO AFFECT YOU DIRECTLY.

harmony, of balance, of an arrangement of forms which in the first
instance may 'simply' please you. Then move forward from there.

MANDALAS AND YANTRAS

You will find examples of the circle, cross, triangle and square in the
patterns known as 'mandalas' and 'yantras'. There is no clear
distinction between these two terms. Both mandalas and yantras are
usually based upon the circle, but whereas mandalas contain
representational figures of gods, humans or animals, yantras are more
usually geometric in design.

One of the best-known yantras is the Sri yantra or Sricakra (wheel
of Sri) shown above. This is a kind of symbolic 'map' of creation. If
you use a mandala or a yantra such as the Sricakra, remember
however that you mustn't concentrate on its meaning or symbolism.
If you do, then you are simply thinking about the symbolism rather
than experiencing what it represents. Instead, allow your mind to go
into the yantra, first by flowing with the movement from the centre
outwards, and then by flowing from the outside back into the centre.

Travel slowly. Try not to move the eyes, but to take in the whole pattern from the one point of vision. Don't think of words even like 'triangle' or 'circle' to describe this journey. Simply follow the shapes.

And as I said when discussing the circle, don't in any case be bounded by the interpretations I've just given. The yantra will reveal meaning to you in other ways. Allow this meaning to arise in its own time and in its own manner. And allow the direct experience of the yantra, with its combination of symbolic shapes, to work its own 'magic' in introducing a harmony and a balance into your life which you may become increasingly aware of as time goes by, yet without quite knowing how it has been achieved.

USING INNER VISION

I indicated earlier that you can travel with pictures not only by observing them directly but by holding them in the mind as visualizations.

If you are one of these people who claim to have little visual imagination, be reassured. Everyone can visualize – we each of us do it every night in dreams. And if you're someone who claims never to dream, be reassured again. We each of us dream every night, and

RIGHT EVERYONE DREAMS AND ANYONE CAN BE TAUGHT HOW TO RECALL THOSE DREAMS IN THE MORNING.

RIGHT THE MASS OF IMAGES THAT BOMBARD US FROM ALL FORMS OF MEDIA HAVE AFFECTED OUR POWERS OF VISUALIZATION.

although some of us never remember our dreams the following morning, with training we can learn to do so.

There are two reasons why some of us find it hard to visualize while we are awake.

Firstly we run up against the old problem of our inability to stay concentrated for any length of time on any one thing.

And secondly we run up against the problem of not enough practice. Unlike previous generations, we have virtually no need to visualize in normal life. Everything is done for us. We are surrounded by images in books, on posters, on films, on the television. Whenever we go sightseeing we carry our cameras around with us – we never have to remember how things look, we simply take photographs of them. And when we aren't taking photographs we're busy buying picture postcards or glossy souvenir books. Before the advent of the camera, people either remembered what they saw, or else they took their sketchbooks or their watercolours with them and created their own pictures.

As a result of this, although we're quite good at remembering words, we're lost when it comes to remembering visual images. And visual images often provide us with much more powerful keys to our inner psychological landscape than does spoken language.

If you are working with a mandala or a yantra, try after a time to commit it to visual memory so completely that you see it in your mind's eye as clearly as if it were hanging on the wall in front of you. In this way the image becomes internalized, as if the boundaries between you and it have disappeared. In this way the image gains power.

Develop your powers of visualization by gazing first at a simple shape, such as the circle or the square or the cross. Gaze at it steadily, without trying to memorize it. Then suddenly snap the eyes shut, and hold the image behind your closed eyelids, almost as if you have taken a photograph of it. Don't worry if the colours change from the real image. The shape is what matters.

Hold it in your mind for as long as you can, but without making too much of an effort. If it drifts away to one side or the other, bring it gently back into the centre. When the image fades, open your eyes and gaze steadily at it once more, then when you feel ready close them and repeat the exercise.

Before very long, you will find that you are able to visualize the shape at will as soon as you close your eyes, even without first gazing at it. Then practise with another shape, and then another. Once you can visualize several shapes easily, play about with them in your mind's eye, combining them and separating them as you please. If by now you can also visualize colours readily, give the shapes colours, and then change the colours.

Work towards the point at which the visualization becomes effortless, and stays at the centre of your visual imagination without wandering off or growing less symmetrical or less distinct. Then and only then go back to your mandala or your yantra and start to work with that in the same way.

TRAVELLING WITH PUZZLES

The human mind is naturally curious; so there is something about a puzzle that sets most of us thinking. We're intrigued to know the answer, and often we worry away at it until we find what that answer is. A puzzle therefore is often a good way of getting us to concentrate, to focus our minds, to start a process not unlike that of meditation.

The difference between this process and meditation is, however, that when solving a puzzle we follow our thoughts instead of just observing them. We use our rational, logical minds. But what happens if our rational, logical minds don't get us anywhere? What happens if the pieces of information contained in the puzzle not only fail to fit together but actually contradict each other? What happens if there is nothing in our store of knowledge that allows us to see why this is and what we should be doing about it? What then?

KOANS

In the Rinzai school of Zen Buddhism, such puzzles are known as 'koans'. The Zen teacher gives the pupil a koan, selected especially for him or her. The pupil goes away and begins searching for the solution. After a time, a solution comes, and the pupil hurries to tell the teacher. The teacher listens to the solution, gives a shake of the head, and sends the pupil away to work harder. The pupil is told to meditate on the koan, to repeat the koan over and over again like a mantra, but with the difference that now one is responding not only to the sound but to the puzzle contained in the sound.

One is told to work on this puzzle with total, single-minded determination, sometimes actively seeking, sometimes simply holding the koan in the mind and waiting to see what comes. But the contemporary Zen teacher Master Sheng-Yen warns:

'Don't try to reason out an answer.
You'll never get it in that way.
You must work on it as if chewing
on nails. You must use it to form in
your mind a hot ball of doubt that
will drive you to find the answer'.

And when the answer comes, the pupil may express it in words, or in gestures, or even in silence. Only the teacher is able to recognize whether the answer is acceptable or not, since such answers are not 'standard' in the way that an examination paper may be standard, and pupils may not always give this answer in what outwardly appears to be the same way.

Sometimes the answers can seem so strange that the dialogue between the teacher and pupil may appear nonsensical. The answer to the koan comes at the point where the mind is driven beyond its rational, 'normal' way of conceptualizing and labelling and categorizing the world. The point at which the mind is driven to experience things directly, without the obscurity which the intellect can place like a veil between us and what actually is.

It is said that through the resolution of koans, Zen can thus take us in a single leap into insight, instead of leaving us first to work through the stages of concentration and tranquillity. It is thus a shortcut on our journey, though there are very few who are able to take it.

WHAT IS THE SOUND OF ONE HAND CLAPPING?

One of the best-known koans, and one which has a particular appeal to the Western mind, is the one I mentioned in chapter 4, 'What is the sound of one hand clapping?' What indeed? What can be the sound of one hand, if by definition clapping is caused by two hands? Could the answer be silence? Hardly, since the koan indicates that 'clapping' is taking place. Well then, can the hand be clapping against itself? If so, could that really be called clapping? And so one goes on. Until one realizes that perhaps this isn't the way one should be travelling at all. In which case, is there another direction? If so, where is it? Or is the whole idea of 'direction' wrong as well?

A Koan from The Hekiganroku

The Hekiganroku is one of the most extensive collections of koans. Here the student is not only given the question and the resolution, but also an introduction and commentary.

Introduction

When the action of the mind is stopped and swept away the iron tree will bloom. Can you demonstrate it? Even a crafty fellow will come a cropper here. Even if he excels in every way, he will have his nostrils pierced. Where are the complications?

Main Subject

Riku Taifu, while talking with Nasen, said 'Jo Hosshi said "Heaven and earth and I are all of the same substance". Isn't that absolutely fantastic?' Nansen pointed to a flower in the garden, called Taifu to him and said 'People of these days see this flower as though they were in a dream'.

Commentary

Hearing, seeing and touching are not one and one. Mountains and rivers should not be viewed in the mirror. The frosty sky, the setting moon – at midnight. With whom will the serene waters of the lake reflect the shadows in the cold?

The introduction sounds like the clue in a crossword puzzle. The Main Subject like a simple statement that people don't really see things properly. And the Commentary, like an attempt in poetry at contradicting Jo Hosshi's statement in the Main Subject. But as the Zen master would say if you offered these solutions to him or her, 'If you think that, you are wrong. And if you don't think that, you are wrong. Now answer!'

OPEN-EYE AND CLOSED-EYE MEDITATION

Working with one's koan is a form of open-eye meditation. One works with it while going about one's ordinary life, while eating, while working, while preparing for sleep. And of course one also works with it in meditation, which in the Zen tradition is usually done with the eyes open.

Meditating with open eyes helps to keep you in touch with this world instead of withdrawing too far into yourself, but closing the eyes has the advantage of developing more rapidly your insight into your own nature. However, whether the path is inner or outer, it leads in the same direction, so neither method is 'better' than the other.

Decide on the method that seems right for you, and use this in your practice. But use the other method too from time to time. Your meditation should enable you to explore both inner and outer space.

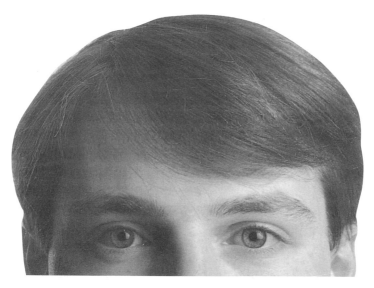

ABOVE THE CHOICE BETWEEN OPEN-EYE AND CLOSE-EYE MEDITATION IS ENTIRELY YOUR OWN, BUT YOU SHOULD CONSIDER THE ADVANTAGES OF BEING ABLE TO PRACTISE IN BOTH WAYS.

EMPTINESS AND ENLIGHTENMENT

In any discussion of meditation, and particularly when ideas like 'emptiness' are mentioned, people are apt to ask about enlightenment.

Does meditation lead to enlightenment? And if so, how does one recognize this enlightenment when it comes?

I've emphasized several times that one doesn't have a 'goal' in meditation, because it would assume that we already 'know' the goal, or at least know what it looks like. But those who meditate for spiritual reasons quite reasonably feel that enlightenment is bound up in some way with meditation, and that the concept is at least in the back of their minds if nowhere else.

So what is enlightenment?

A clue is given to us in the third stage of the meditation practice: insight. Enlightenment is insight into reality, the direct experience of things as they are. What else could it be?

This means that instead of thinking of enlightenment as a single blinding flash of revelation (though of course it could be that), it may be more helpful to think of it as a step-by-step process, a number of enlightenment experiences. As we gain insight into the physical body, into the emotions, into the mind, and into the emptiness from which form emerges and into which form returns, we are going deeper and deeper into a direct experience of reality, an experience which may bring us in time to a profound spiritual realization of the nature of our own existence and of the existence of all other created things.

But if we set out deliberately to achieve this realization, then our very deliberateness, with all the mental concepts that it contains, and our very preoccupation with achievement, may serve as the barriers which come between it and us.

CONTEMPLATION

This section would not be complete without some reference to contemplation, a practice which, among Western Christians in particular, is often confused with meditation.

Contemplation carries different meanings for different people but essentially it involves an inner thought process centred around some important idea. For example, one could contemplate such statements as 'God is love' or one of the ten commandments or Buddhist precepts. The mind examines the statement from every point of view, trying to obtain insight into its true meaning.

Such a practice differs importantly from meditation in that it uses thought processes and emotional responses, rather than just observing them. However, contemplation is a very valuable practice, and can lead not only to a fuller understanding of the statement contemplated but also to sudden flashes of profound insight.

As I said earlier, we must never think less of thought itself simply because in meditation we are freeing ourselves from thought and experiencing the underlying reality from which thought arises. Thought is a powerful and vital tool of the mind, and only causes us problems when we assume that it *is the mind.*

You may wonder nevertheless how contemplation differs from koan meditation, which also takes its starting point from a statement. The difference is that in koan meditation we are working with a statement that we are trying in some sense to 'resolve'. And to do so, moreover, without the use of thought or emotion. We may certainly begin with thought and/or with emotion, but there comes a point where these drop away, and the answer comes as a moment of pure experience. In contemplation on the other hand, the aim is usually to work by means of thought and emotion.

It is also true that whereas meditation involves a relatively specific set of practices, contemplation is a state into which we enter whenever we ponder the meaning of a statement by an advanced teacher, or the line of a poem, or the atmosphere captured by a painting or by a piece of music. It does not usually involve either the 'discipline' inseparable from meditation, or the consistent use of the same point of focus.

DISTRACTIONS IN MEDITATION

From the start of your meditation, you will experience distractions. Few meditators ever become completely free from them. And the fact that we seem to be able to ignore them in one meditation is no guarantee we'll be able to ignore them next time around. In fact this

BELOW THE SOUND OF CHILDREN PLAYING SHOULD NOT BE SEEN AS A DISTRACTION, BUT AS PART OF THE REALITY THAT YOU ARE LOOKING AT DURING MEDITATION.

up and down nature of meditation can be a major distraction in itself. We become frustrated with ourselves, and fed up with meditation, and these angry feelings are a further barrier between us and what we are trying to do.

The golden rule is always just to sit through whatever comes up. Without realizing it, we often make more progress during those meditations where we have to work hard to stay concentrated than in those where concentration comes easily.

WHAT TO DO ABOUT DISTRACTIONS

People naturally ask what should they do when the noise of traffic in the streets, or of the television next door, or of children playing in the garden starts to disturb their tranquillity. Equally they ask what should they do when legs start to ache, when noses start to itch, when a foot goes to sleep, when the tune of a popular song maddeningly starts playing over and over again in the brain. The answer each time can only be 'simply observe it'. This is more easily said than done of course. But remember that meditation is not an 'escape' from reality, it is a 'looking at' reality. And the distractions both outside and inside the mind are part of that reality.

So don't try and ignore distractions, don't try and push them away. Don't react to them. Accept them as part of the flow of experience.

When meditating with a teacher in certain forms of meditation practice, he or she lets out a fierce and penetrating yell, or smacks two pieces of wood together at certain unpredictable points. These intrusions into one's meditation come violently, almost brutally. The sound tears into the meditator, deliberately shattering his or her tranquillity into a thousand pieces.

Or does it? Is tranquillity really shattered? If it is, then it isn't true tranquillity. If the meditator has been shut off into a cosy inner world, imagining it to be tranquillity, the impact of the sound quickly shows the state for what it was. If one jumps out of one's skin, one certainly wasn't in a state of tranquillity. But if one was, then the sound is accepted by the mind simply as a sound, a sound which helps the meditator to see more deeply into the true nature of experience.

So although in the early days of your meditation practice you may find it necessary to have silence around you, as you progress you will become more and more able to sit with noises from outside, recognizing them as a part of your mind (or, if you prefer, as part of what is happening in your mind). But this still leaves the problem of the pain in the leg or the itch on the nose or the pins and needles in the foot. What do you do? Shift into a more comfortable position? Scratch the nose? Rub the foot back into life?

It isn't a crime to do any of these things and you should never turn your meditation into a trial, which has to be endured come what may. But the stillness of the body is important, since it helps to still the mind. Also important is the realization that if you are uncomfortable now and shift to ease your discomfort, you will feel uncomfortable again in a few minutes. Also, by trying to 'escape' from your discomfort, you are missing the opportunity to learn from it.

So sit through your discomfort if you can. Don't try and push it away or ignore it. But don't concentrate on it either. Concentrating on it only gives it added importance. Note it, observe it, see what the physical sensation actually is (as opposed to giving it a label or judging it in some way), and continue with your practice. Eventually, your meditation will embrace all these distractions, seeing them as part of the moment by moment flow of experience.

MEDITATION IN DAILY LIFE

I have stressed many times that meditation isn't an escape from reality, but a way of dealing with it, of gaining insight into it. This being the case, meditation shouldn't be confined just to those times when you can sit and practice. Meditation should be something that can be carried through into daily life, even reaching the point where life itself becomes a meditation. If this sounds impossibly over idealistic, or as if you are expected to go through life like a monk or nun, rest assured. It's nothing of the kind. It means only that you will be able to bring something of the concentration, the relaxed focused attention of your sitting practice, into the wider business of living.

Much of the time we go through our lives in a dream, our minds are always on something other than what we are doing. This leads to stress and forgetfulness. The lessons learnt in meditation help us to overcome this, helping us to put our minds in the moment, to experience directly instead of being lost in the distractions of thoughts.

MINDFULNESS

Much of this increased concentration comes naturally once we take up the practice of meditation. But our concentration can also be improved by just observing what is happening to us and around us all of the time.

This practice, called 'mindfulness', is the exact opposite of absent-mindedness. It doesn't mean that we should never daydream, it means that we should always know what we are doing. If we choose to go into a daydream that is fine – they can be very helpful. But we shouldn't just sink into it out of habit.

A simple technique for helping you to remain mindful is to keep a running commentary in your head about what you are

111

RIGHT WHEN YOU ARE OUT WALKING, TAKE NOTICE OF EVERYTHING THAT SURROUNDS YOU – THIS WILL HELP TO DEVELOP MINDFULNESS.

WATCHFULNESS IN THE BUDDHIST *DHAMMAPADA*

Watchfulness is the path of immortality: unwatchfulness is the path of death.

Those who are watchful never die: those who do not watch are already as dead.

---

doing. This makes you concentrate, makes you put your mind in your actions, makes you notice things around you, makes you properly aware and attentive. If you are forced to break off one action halfway through in order to start on something else, it records the fact for you, and helps you remember where you were in the first action. The result is that you can return to this action as soon as possible and pick it up again at the point at which you left it.

Try this running commentary for a few minutes at a time, several times a day. Allow it to include awareness of your own thoughts and feelings as you react to what is going on around you. Try it when you are harassed and attempting to do 101 things at once. Try it when you are out walking or driving, so that it makes you use your eyes and take in the things around you. Try it when you're doing something boring like washing dishes, and when the mind is prone to go wandering off on its own. It will help train your mind, so that after a time you will find yourself paying attention to life even when the commentary isn't going on inside your head.

Mindfulness helps you be more effective and better organized, but it does more than that. It continues the process of insight that you are developing in your sitting meditation. It helps you become more aware of what it is to be alive, of the nature of reality, of events in the outside world and of your reactions to them. It is no accident that so many of the great spiritual traditions place emphasis upon mindfulness.

ACHIEVING SPECIFIC GOALS

I discussed earlier in the chapter the way in which you can use simple visualization as a point of focus in meditation. Once you have developed your ability both to concentrate and to visualize clearly, you can use visualization in other ways too. This is quite a different thing to your usual meditation practice. You are now setting out to achieve specific, clearly defined goals. The exercises should be used in addition to your usual meditation practice, not in place of it.

VISUALIZATION FOR THE BODY

Let's start by seeing how visualization can help with a physical problem, such as a bad back. The nagging pain and the restriction of movement caused by the problem quickly lead the sufferer to think of him or herself as a person moving slowly and stiffly through life. As a result their self-image becomes that of a person with a bad back.

The result of this negative self-image is that the individual sees him or herself in terms of disability rather than ability. Not only does this have a depressing effect on the mind (which in itself makes recovery difficult), it results in the body becoming full of tension, making healing a greater struggle. A simple visualization exercise, carried out for a few minutes once or twice a day, when combined with the appropriate medical treatment, can help the sufferer to break out of this vicious circle. In the exercise, the individual pictures him or herself free from pain and able to move with freedom.

VISUALIZATION FOR THE MIND

Visualizations can help the mind as well as the body. Just as a negative physical self-image interferes with physical well-being, so a negative psychological self-image interferes with psychological well-being.

If we constantly think of ourselves as shy for example, or as depressed or over-anxious, then we are conditioning ourselves to be shy or depressed or over-anxious. We need to replace self-images of this kind with positive ones of the person we want to be.

When dealing with a psychological problem, you should again use a visualization of yourself, this time coping confidently with a situation that has previously proved difficult for you.

Visualize the situation in as much detail as you can. Visualize the other people who may be there, and 'hear' what they are likely to say. Now imagine yourself identifying with and moving inside the visualization of your confident self, so that you and it become one, and you feel the relaxed energy with which this self is dealing with the problem. Alternatively if you're depressed, visualize yourself in good spirits (talking to friends, taking a favourite walk), and then become one with this happy self.

VISUALIZATION FOR THE SPIRIT

Spiritually, we can also help by visualizing ourselves as having those qualities we need for our further development. We may therefore choose to visualize a spiritual teacher. The image symbolizes for the meditator the qualities he or she wishes to develop, and when the visualization stands out clearly in the mind, the meditator visualizes these desirable qualities as streaming rays of white light into his or her own being.

114

VISUALIZATION TECHNIQUES

There are many different ways in which you can use visualizations for physical, psychological or spiritual purposes, but the principle behind them all is relatively simple. Use your visual imagination to create a picture of what it is you want to become. The clearer and more convincing the picture, and the more closely you identify with it, the more likely are you to be successful.

In the case of physical problems, the aim is to visualize yourself as free from these problems, or to visualize yourself as fighting and defeating them. The visualizations can be of two main kinds:

EXERCISE 7

This exercise can be carried out lying down (though you can sit in your meditation position if you prefer). Keep the mind alert, just as usual.

Allow the body to relax. Let your awareness sweep the body, as in meditation, letting go of any tensions which you may find.

Create an image of a peaceful scene, say a sandy beach. Keep the visualization simple. Concentrate upon the long sweep of sand, upon the sea breaking in gentle waves upon the shore, on the blue sunlit sky.

Visualize birds soaring and swooping above you. Be conscious of the freedom of their movement, of their grace and relaxed beauty.

Visualize a human figure, yourself in light clothing or naked, running and dancing with the same freedom and grace along the shoreline. See your feet throwing up a spray of water that sparkles in the sun. Notice how pain free and unrestricted you are, how your body can leap and twist and turn as it pleases.

Now put your consciousness inside that body, so that you feel this freedom from inside. Feel the sun on your body, the sand and the water beneath your feet, the warm air as you run through it, the ease with which your back allows you to do as you please, to bend and stretch, to relax into the joy of movement.

Allow this to continue for as long as you wish.

EXERCISE 7 (CONTINUED)

When you are ready, withdraw from the visualization, so that you are lying once more in your room but still feeling the freedom and sheer exhilaration of movement in your body.

Then dissolve the visualization of the scene in front of you, allowing the running figure and the sea and the sky and the beach to be absorbed into you rather than vanish. Tell yourself that you will be able to return to the scene whenever you want.

Don't be tempted to leap up now as if your back has received instant healing. Behave sensibly, but keep the feeling of relaxation in the muscles and nerves of the back, and the realization that healing is taking place. Nature knows her own business best. Once we give her the chance, she will do the healing for us.

These same principles can be used for any other physical or psychological problem, but do remember that they are additional to, not an alternative to qualified medical advice.

116

- An outer visualization, such as yourself running joyfully and pain free along a beach or through a wood or wherever you choose.

- An inner visualization, such as your white blood corpuscles defeating an infection, or torn muscles or ligaments healing.

In addition you can 'feel' yourself moving freely or in whatever state it is you want to achieve. Identify fully with the feeling. Imagine yourself becoming one with the visualization of yourself running along the beach, and sensing the joy of movement as if it is actually happening to you, here and now, in this moment. Exercise 7 gives a brief example, using a bad back as the point of focus.

As with all work of this kind, never be impatient. We're so conditioned to expect quick results (a magic pill that will put everything to rights) that we expect to experience the desired effects after only a few minutes of visualization. You will need to work for 20 minutes a day for some time (weeks, perhaps months) before the benefits will begin to show. Even then, success isn't guaranteed. Or it may come in an unexpected form. For example, you may find you begin to understand your physical disability or your psychological problem better, to understand why it is there and what it is perhaps trying to teach you. Or you may find yourself more tolerant of it, gentler and less impatient with it, better able to cope.

Don't be discouraged if your progress seems slow. When you come to hills, progress is bound to be a little slower.

117

GUIDES AND COMPANIONS

You will sometimes hear it said that you cannot make progress in meditation without a teacher. This is true. But perhaps not in the sense in which you at first imagine. For you are your own best teacher. Other people can help, particularly if they have trodden the path you are now treading, and know some of the snares and pitfalls. They can encourage you, listen to your accounts of progress or setbacks, advise you when to move from one practice to another, give you koans and other travellers' aids. But remember that they cannot take your journey for you. In the end, you are the one who travels, and you are the one who must find the path.

BOOKS

Books can also be a great help. Some meditation teachers will tell you that you can't learn from books, but these are usually teachers very much influenced by Eastern traditions, where books and their power are not always as well known and appreciated as in the West. It is true that you can't learn just by reading books. You must put into practice what they teach. Books are not a substitute for practice, but then they are not meant to be. They are guides to set you on your way, travelling companions to help you recognize your path when you find it. They can motivate, arouse interest, even inspire, and by placing the onus upon yourself rather than upon a teacher who is physically present with you, they can help you to be more self-reliant, readier to explore, more aware of the personal nature of what it is you are trying to do.

TEACHERS

On the other hand, if you find a good teacher he or she can answer individual queries, listen to your grumbles and help you through periods when you may not feel you are making progress. You look at your teacher and admire his or her open, optimistic, serene approach to life, and you think that if that is what meditation can do for them, then certainly it is something worth having.

But how do you find a good teacher? Since of all the great religions, Buddhism places most emphasis upon meditation, you may find a good meditation teacher by identifying a Buddhist group near you and contacting them; your local town or college library will probably have details, or you can get the addresses of all the larger Buddhist centres from such sources as the Buddhist Society. Alternatively, you may find a yoga teacher who takes meditation classes. Or you may

119

BELOW IF YOU FIND A TEACHER WHO INSPIRES YOU AND WITH WHOM YOU CAN DISCUSS ANY QUESTIONS OR PROBLEMS THAT ARISE, YOUR MEDITATION PRACTICE IS SURE TO BENEFIT.

wish to work through a Transcendental Meditation (TM) group where the emphasis is upon a simple mantra meditation. But if you find the philosophy surrounding any of these groups unacceptable to you, there is no reason at all why you shouldn't continue to work on your own.

In my own experience of a wide range of meditation teachers over the years I have invariably found that those who helped me most were those who were open to experience rather than firmly located in one set of beliefs. Remember, in meditation as in all of life, no one has a monopoly of the truth. And if they try to tell you they have, then avoid them and their teachings.

THE MEDITATION RETREAT

At some point, you may feel you want a more intensive experience of meditation, spread over a few days or even weeks. This means you are ready for a meditation retreat, either in the company of others or on your own.

A number of traditions, both Christian and Buddhist, operate retreat centres or monasteries where retreats can be taken, but a 'retreat' can mean a number of different things. It can mean a study weekend where periods of meditation are interspersed with teaching and discussion sessions. Or it can mean a period of time where, though you are in the company of others, you are left to decide for yourself when and how you want to practise. Or it can be an intensive silent retreat with a full timetable of meditation sessions starting early in the morning and going on into the evening, with short breaks only for silent meals or for work periods.

If you decide to go on a retreat, be sure you know what you are letting yourself in for before you go. Don't take on too much too soon. All retreats demand a degree of discipline, but you should feel able to sit for several 20- or 30-minute sessions a day before you enrol on one.

The great value of a retreat is that it allows you, through the intensity of your practice, to develop concentration, tranquillity and insight more rapidly than you would otherwise be able to do. In the first day or two of a retreat you many feel nothing is happening, but by the third day you many find yourself in a still state which penetrates both your meditation and the periods between meditation. However, though retreats are a great help, they are no substitute for regular daily practice. Some people return from a retreat feeling they have at last made progress; then, struck by the 'dullness' of routine sitting they cease to do anything until the next retreat. This is a major mistake. Retreats are there to add to your daily practice, not to replace it. They are times for taking stock, for getting a further perspective on where you are, for exploring more fully the potential of what it is you are doing when you sit to practice. But they do take place away from everyday life, and the real test of where you are is still your daily routine, and the extent to which you can find a space within it for meditation.

Conclusion

Some journeys have a definite destination, and when you arrive at it you know you have arrived. Other journeys are different. You set off not knowing quite where you are going or why, but knowing it is a journey you want to or feel you must take. You carry with you the few things you think you're going to need, and then find bit by bit that most of these can be left behind too.

Meditation is the second kind of journey. Now that you have come this far, some of the scenery is familiar to you. There are landmarks which you recognize, and which open out and welcome you. Sometimes you seem to be going back in the direction from which you came, at other times you seem to be covering a great deal of ground very quickly. There are surprises. Unexpected experiences, some of them encouraging, some of them disconcerting. And always in the distance there are the far hills and the trees on the horizon. It is possible that the journey of meditation has no end, that the path, like space and time, is infinite. Or it is possible that the destination is yourself, and that you and that infinity are one. No matter. Concentrate upon travelling with hope and with courage, and your meditation will not fail you. I wish you peace and joy on your journey, and the kindness of friends as your blessing.

FURTHER READING

A number of authorities are mentioned or quoted in the text. Below is a selection of their work and other books which will help you in your study of meditation. Some explanatory details are given on each.

Arnold, E. *The Light of Asia*, Routledge & Kegan Paul, 1971. A long poem on the life, character and philosophy of the Buddha; full of profound insights beautifully expressed.

Bancroft, A. *Zen: Direct Pointing at Reality*, Thames and Hudson, 1979. A beautifully illustrated survey of many Zen practices, including walking meditation.

Blofeld, J. *Mantras: Sacred Words of Power*, Unwin, 1977. Available as a Mandala paperback, this is one of the best short introductions to the meaning and power of the mantra.

Blyth, R. H. *A History of Haiku* (2 vols), Hokuseido Press, 1964. An excellent, definitive survey of haiku poetry. Published in Tokyo, it is still in print but may be difficult to obtain.

Carrington, P. *Managing Meditation in Clinical Practice*, in M. West (ed.) *The Psychology of Meditation*, Oxford University Press, 1987. A thorough survey of many of the medical and psychological benefits of meditation.

Chögyam, Ngakpa *Journey into Vastness*, Element Books, 1988. Excellent introduction to Tibetan meditational practices, including shi-ne.

Conze, E. *Buddhist Meditation*, Unwin, 1972. One of the most readily available sources for the Buddha's own teaching on vipassana.

Cooper, J. C. *An Illustrated Encyclopedia of Traditional Symbols*, Thames and Hudson, 1978. A must for all those interested in symbols and their significance. A scholarly but highly readable work, profusely illustrated, and now available as a large-format paperback.

Eliot, T. S. *Collected Poems 1909–1962*, Faber & Faber, 1963. Of all modern Western poets, Eliot had the surest grasp of mystical experience, and combined an understanding of both Western and Eastern spirituality. Available in paperback.

French, R. M. (translator) *The Way of a Pilgrim*, SPCK, 1942. A classic of Christian meditational literature using the Jesus prayer. Available in paperback.

Govinda, Lama Anagarika *Creative Meditation and Multi-dimensional Consciousness*, Unwin, 1977. Available as a Mandala paperback. Not an easy book, but richly rewarding. Deals with colours as well as mantras and mandalas.

Herrigel, E. *Zen in the Art of Archery*, Routledge, 1953. A classic, as perfect as a Zen painting or a haiku poem. In R. F. C. Hull's beautiful translation from the German, the book says more in each sentence than most books say in their whole length. Continuously in print and now available as an Arkana paperback.

Jung, C. *Memories, Dreams, Reflections*, Fontana, 1967. The autobiography of the Western psychologist most in tune with the psychological value of meditation. Now available as a Fount paperback.

Mascaro, J. (translator) *The Dhammapada*, Penguin, 1973. One of the great spiritual classics of world literature.

McDonald, K. *How to Meditate*, Wisdom, 1984. A very practical guide to the use, among other things, of the visualization of the Buddha - or other spiritual teachers-in meditation.

Sekida, K. (translator) *Two Zen Classics: Mumonkan and Hekiganroku*, Weatherhill, 1977. Two of the most mind-baffling collections of koans. Perhaps the ultimate experience in Zen literature.

Sheng-Yen, *Master Getting the Buddha Mind*, Dharma Drum Publications, 1982. The teachings of a modern Ch'an master during a meditation retreat.

Simonton, O.C. Mathews-Simonton, S. and Creighton, J.L. *Getting Well Again*, Bantam Books, 1980. An excellent introduction to the use of visualizations for healing and health.

Suzuki, D. T. *Essays in Zen Buddhism* (3 vols), Rider, 1953. One of the best of the many publications produced by the man who first made Zen comprehensible to the West.

Van de Wetering, J. *A Glimpse of Nothingness*, Routledge, 1979. First-hand account of experiences in an American Zen community.

INDEX

127